Towards the Inside

MENAKA NEOTIA

Book Title: Towards the Inside
Book Author: Menaka Neotia

This edition published June 2020

ISBN 9781660553396
ASIN 1660553393

With deep gratitude to Marshall B. Rosenberg

AUTHOR'S PREFACE

"I want to share it this with as many people as possible, in the hopes of managing to inspire enough people to rise up to make it happen." - Miki Kashtan

This novella was born first, as a screenplay that I wrote when I started working with an NGO called Hazards Centre in New Delhi in 2015. The founder - Dunu Roy, told me about the plight of the Bengali speaking waste-pickers, and how they are illegally detained and deported to Bangladesh. I had just returned from the US after doing a course at The Lee Strasberg Film and Theatre Institute, and so I wrote it as a screenplay, hoping that it would turn into a feature film someday. That's why the stories and research took the shape of being set in a fiction story, even though I researched for it, for almost 8 months with the guidance of Dunu Roy and Dilip Simeon Labour Historian, to write the first draft. While I was also working with the waste-picker community at Ghazipur, during my time at the Hazards Centre.

I am not a trained book writer, and I couldn't find someone to edit my book for no charge at this time. So, I have gone ahead and skipped editing, and got my book proof-read and published it, as I want to put all the stories and research out there. It had been lying with me since 2015, evolving with my experiences as, I also began my journey of practicing Nonviolent Communication (NVC) in 2015, NVC is a process created by Marshall B. Rosenberg. While creating the process of NVC, Marshall who saw the violence in the world, chose to see the beauty and compassion that exists in every human. From 2015 as my learning in NVC grew, with practice sometimes the lens with which I started seeing our issues in our world shifted to a more compassionate view of it, and I have included those in the book. And it is this, that I hope will touch the minds of readers. I long to inspire humans to take self-responsibility, and I can tell you that it won't be easy, and also that it'll be the most enjoyable choice you would ever make in your life, you will feel alive and that has been the realist experience for me in my living.

I want to live in a world where everyone's needs matter and most needs are met. Yes, this is possible. It is possible for most needs to be met in a collaborative society. Only a large number of people can create a world where there is an absence of the desire and the need to do harm. If you want self-connection and connection with others, you will have to make a conscious choice, become aware, and practice it. Change is not just going to happen, we are the world we are the change.

Several ways can lead to the cultivation of compassion, which enhances the possibility of connection with the humanness in every person, with uncompromising presence, the ones that I have heard of and/or been in the practice of, coming to me at this time are -- Vipassana and Process Work develop the practice of connecting with feelings, Restorative Justice Circle restores every person to their humanness, Species and Environmental Restoration have the intention of preservation and coexisting, Al-anon for family and friends of alcoholics for self-care and empathy, and Nonviolent Communication (NVC). NVC is the only process I know of at this time that connects with feelings and dips into needs to create collaborative nonviolent realities for all. This book is an attempt to share my experience living in NVC consciousness because I think that if there is a shift in our collective awareness, we would be knowing and willing to create collaborative nonviolent futures for all!

Menaka Neotia, New Delhi, May 2020

Standing in front of a garbage truck, holding a clapboard front of the filming camera, the clap boy says loudly — "Scene 18, shot 4, take 4," — and sounds clap.

Prem Ratan -- a successful Bollywood filmmaker is directing the film. He is also an artist— creates storyboard, does cinematography, set design, and also composes music for his films. And he also contributes as a cartoonist in a leading news daily— Chimes of India. Prem Ratan lives in his surreal world, and whenever he speaks it sounds like he is saying dialogues from a film-script.

The camera is rolling and capturing Hero No. 1 and Heroine No. 1. The camera zooms into the front window of a truck, where we can see Hero No. 1 and Heroin No. 1-- seated in the front seat of a garbage truck, exchanging subtle love glances, while a love song in Hindi plays in the background.

'Kai baar yun bhi tum dekho,
yeh kachra nahin, mera dil hai..'

The film camera zooms out, and we get to see Heroine No. 2 clenching one of her fists together, close to her mouth.

.   .   .

Self-resonance Diary. Note 1. I have been reading the history of Assam, the Partition of India-Pakistan, and West Pakistan-East Pakistan and the life of the people in the Brahmaputra Valley in Assam, India. I can sense a whirlpool inside my stomach. My throat starts throbbing. Anuradha, is your heart beating faster? My breathing is getting hard. Do you notice how leaders often overlook the implications that the administrative decisions and changes can have on the very existence of people? The British signed a treaty with Burma and Burma had to pay an indemnity of one million pounds sterling, back in 1826. Do you feel overwhelmed? Torn maybe? Do you know that in the scale of human history that was the era of colonising? You sense some pins and needles in the head, the history is old -- old and long. Reading also about British administration, they were committed, bookkeepers. They annexed Assam and separated the largely Muslim eastern areas from the largely Hindu western areas by territorially reorganising the Bengal Presidency. Anuradha, did they think about the implications? The division would have had on the culture and life of humans for generations after generations. It brought out fears, and longings for security, belonging, and trust maybe? Can humans be valued over administrative efficiency? Or can we look for ways to care for the needs of humans while thinking of administrative strategies? In the human history scale we are now perhaps in the eras of Democracy and Authoritarian Governance and Neoliberal Capitalism, which you have heard Noam Chomsky say -- has been there since 1920. You long that we are ready to move to another stage in our human history, and wondering how many people will be willing to try something new? You have been reading a book my Miki Kashtan and her suggestion about creating Nonviolent Collaborative Systems is resonating with every cell in your body. Her book suggests systemic changes and for that, we have to have the courage of also changing the systems that we are already involved in. You remember the words of your aunt when she took the sari from your hand, "Let my daughter choose first." Do you want to have the courage to step out of the conditioning, that you have to put others needs first, and your own needs don't matter, be the better person, and lovingly say, "I hear you have a need to consider your daughter's choices, and would you be willing to consider mine too?" I let out a long exhale. Shared-realities, aliveness, and the absence of the need to harm! Togetherness and resonance for all, Anuradha.

OCTOBER 6, 2015
MORNING
DHAKA - BANGLADESH

It is a restful morning, the sun is bright. Anuradha is facing her kitchen window and sunlight graces Anuradha's face, which makes her face glow. Bano the domestic worker is washing dishes in a corner, where sunlight doesn't reach her.

…beethe din, kaise beeti ratiyaaaaa, piya jaane na hayeee… Anuradha hums a Hindi film song while reaching out to a vessel to make tea in, she turns around to Bano, "Chai?" Bano nods a yes. Hot bubbles of water, twirling in it is a cloud of milk. One can hear pounding thud thud thud thud.. blah blah… Tea is ready. Anuradha strains the tea into two cups, "Come to the room with the swing, once you are done with the dishes, okay?" Bano gives a quick reluctant nod.

.　　　.　　　.

Anuradha turns on the radio and sits on one side of the swing, hanging down from the ceiling of her drawing-room.

"Welcome this is RJ Ron, I went to America to become an actor, but came right back to you in Bangladesh when I found my calling to be an RJ, you can hear me connect with you on my show Speak Spice only on 96.4 Spice FM.
Today we have with us a 6 member band called Nadīra Mānuṣa meaning the River People in Bengali! They are a modern rock band, influenced by western music. And they do vocals in Bengali. They use instruments like the Bashi which is a flute made of bamboo, Dhol which is a

percussion instrument, Ektara - a single-stringed instrument, Dotara - a four-stringed instrument, and Mandira - a pair of metal bowls used for rhythm effect," looking at the band members, "the members of your band work with the Sapori people living in the char areas of the Brahmaputra river, tell us something about your work with them?"

"Our work began in 2005 with the Brahmaputra Boat Clinic, a mobile medical unit that can reach the islanders not only in emergencies but to provide the kind of basic, routine care like immunisations that the Sapori people, disconnected from the mainland's infrastructure, usually have lacked."

"You talked about those championing anti-erosion strategies in an interview, could you say more about that?"

"Well, what struck us is that they rarely ask the people living on the islands and river banks for their opinions. It's not just..."

Bano enters and goes and stands behind Anuradha to the right of the wooden swing suspended with brass chains with brass peacocks on it.

"I'm done, di" Anuradha is startled, she turns around and finds Bano hidden behind the darkness that consumes the other side of the swing. Tapping at the swing, Anuradha asks Bano to come to have tea. Bano moves to the swing trying to grab her teacup, but Anuradha is lightly moving the swing with her feet. Bano tries again to quickly leap forward and grab the teacup, but the swing moves back, she gets ready to try a third time when the swing moves toward her, she leaps and misses it, she is about to leap the fourth time when Anuradha turns around, watches Bano leap forward and then move back, Anuradha stops the swing and gives Bano an amused look. Bano quickly picks up her teacup and is about to squat on the floor.

"Arrey sit on top, here," Anuradha taps the swing.

"No di" gesturing she is fine with her hand and squats on the floor.

Anuradha senses her discomfort on seeing Bano down on the floor, while she is up on the swing, her longing for equality, respect and a need to understand personal boundaries is burning inside her, she turns to face Bano, "how is Masira doing now?" Bano says that she has been asked to rest for 2 more days.

"What are you going to do when Masira joins back work here?"

Bano says that she doesn't know.

"Why did you come here from Assam?" Bano is an Assamese speaking Muslim from Dhubri which is in Assam. Her ancestors were taken to Assam from West Bengal to work in tea estates. Bano says that they are D-Voters.

"D-voters?"

Bano tells her that she has voted twice, but now they sent her here, saying that she's Bangladeshi.

"Why didn't you show your identity papers for proof of being an Indian?"

Bano says their name didn't come in the register.

"What does that mean?"

Bano shrugs her shoulders, "Anu di, Masira told me you are also from India? Your name also didn't come in the register?"

Anuradha pauses to think. Then responds, "my baba moved to India before the war and we have been granted Indian citizenship," pauses and continues, "my father saw his brother's head get chopped off before he fled to India. I was born in Bangalore, in the South. I grew big and wanted to become a film actor, but since it was difficult to get work in Bollywood, and my baba knew people in Bangladesh, he sent me to Dhallywood to act in films."

Bano is thrilled to know that Anuradha is an actor, "are you filmi?!"

Anuradha knows that what Masira means by asking if she is filmi is that if she acts in films, and laughs thinking that she is filmi which in Hindi could mean she is like a drama-queen of sorts, Anuradha asks her what her name is?

"Bano, Mahjabeen Bano."

Anuradha exclaims, "whoa! that was Meena Kumari's real name, that means you are Choti Bahu!"

Bano looks lost.

"Arrey, Meena Kumari's film Sahib Biwi Aur Ghulam you have seen?"

Bano replies, "haan di I have seen all her films."

Anuradha reminds her that Meena Kumari was called 'Choti Bahu' meaning younger brother's wife, in that film.

"Oh, haan she is Choti Bahu in that pichar!" both laugh. Pichar is a Hindi word for a feature film.

OCTOBER 12, 2015

Anuradha's manager Debarshi Das aka Debu has been working with Anuradha for several years. He is watching TV in his office. A reporter asks Prem Ratan, "Why did you choose this topic?"

Prem Ratan replies, "Because it has great contemporary relevance, not only in our country but all over the world!"

"When will the film's shooting begin?"

"There's time for that, now we are going to Delhi for a location recce."

"Why did you choose Delhi?"

"During the research, we got to know that many of the illegal immigrants also work as waste-pickers, their bastis are in Delhi."

Debu gets an idea, mutes the TV and calls Anuradha. Debu tells Anuradha about Prem Ratan's film. He gives her an idea to do a charity event in Delhi, with Prem Ratan as the chief guest. Anuradha thinks it is a brilliant idea. Debu looks for NGOs working with waste-pickers in Delhi, Sahyog Kendra's name pops up in one of the search results. He reads up about them. They have done extensive work all over India. He notes down their contact number.

.   .   .

OCTOBER 16, 2015
SAHYOG KENDRA
NEW DELHI - INDIA

Vikram founded Sahyog Kendra 35 years ago in Delhi to offer consultancy and support on a community approach basis, on matters related to livelihoods, housing, education, health, etc.

Firoza, the graphic designer sitting behind Vikram is working on a poster with the following words written on it, 'DIVERSITY IS HAVING A SEAT AT THE TABLE, INCLUSION IS HAVING A VOICE, AND BELONGING IS HAVING THAT VOICE BE HEARD.'

Firoza stretches and calls out to two girls sitting to her right, and asks them, "One day when Amitabh Bachan and his son Abhishek Bachan were traveling in a ricksha, what did Amitabh tell Abhishek?"

They reply, "No idea."

She says, "one minute let's ask Vikram," and calls out to Vikram. Vikram turns around, she asks him, "Vikram, one day Amitabh Bachan and… what did he tell Abhishek?"

Vikram asks, "What did he say, Bhai?" Bhai is like saying 'bro' in Hindi.

She completes the sentence, "rickshe mein toh hum tumhare baap lagte hai!" in a rickshaw, I am like your father, both the girls cover their mouth and start giggling.

Vikram asks "what is so funny?"

Firoza asks him, "have you seen the film Shahenshah?"

Vikram says, "no," - his phone starts ringing.

Priyanka, Tahir Bhai, and Midori are sitting in front of Vikram in the centre of the office room, facing each other, in a circle. Midori is Japanese studying in China and has approached Sahyog Kendra, as she is doing a study on immigrant women. She is discussing the interview she had with an immigrant lady the previous day. Midori can speak in English and needed someone to translate from Hindi to English for her, so Priyanka who works in the Media and communication team at Sahyog Kendra goes with Midori for her interviews.

Midori, "I was telling Priyanka to ask her if she is married, or did she just sleep with those men for money? I knew she was lying about being married."

Tahir Bhai asks her, "But why you think she was choosing to lie about marriage?"

Midori quickly reacts, "see- see I knew she was lying…"
Tahir Bhai tries to explain, "Madem she is maybis needing for her safety and integrity no, that's why she maybis telling she is married…"

Tahir Bhai was a homeless boy when Vikram spotted him on the street, Tahir Bhai was looking at getting work and wanted to study at the same time, Vikram guided him throughout his days on the street. Now Tahir Bhai works with immigrants and is trying to get them together, to be able to mobilise them and ask them how they would like to stand up for their rights.

The office help Shambhuji, is a healthy-looking person, serves tea to Midori, and the others, they take their teacups, and ask him, "arrey Shambhuji, come sit with us?"

Shambhuji slowly pulls up a chair and sits with them, and informs them that he is leaving to go to the bank, in a while. And asks them to wash their teacups. They agree.

Vikram puts the phone down and calls out to Zublin. He asks Zublin to get Anuradha's charity event organised. Zublin asks him if he should contact Guru Bhai? "Why are you involving him in all this? Why don't you call the municipality, and talk to them instead?"

Zublin has been working with Sahyog Kendra for 4 years. He is from Delhi and went to study at the Tata Institute of Social Sciences in Bombay for 2 years before joining Sahyog Kendra.

.   .   .

DECEMBER 16, 2015

Anuradha and Debu come to Delhi for the charity event. Punjabi rap music with dhol and jembe plays from their cab stereo, 'Pairi pauna pauji,' meaning touching the feet of an elder person... A bus moves in front of their cab, the poster behind the bus reads, 'Dilli bole dil se, odd-even fir se.' Everyone comes to a halt, the bus has slowed down in the middle of the road, a person hailing the bus runs and quickly gets inside the bus. Bus jerks and moves fast. Sound of water being pumped out, Anuradha looks outside her moving cab's window, a person is pumping out water from a 'thande paani ka thela,' which is a cold water dispenser, outside Islamic Center which has a blue mosaic dome. 'Pee paww pee paww,' sound of an ambulance which is stuck in traffic, right outside the hospital.

The charity event is at Indian Institute Centre. Prem Ratan is impressed with the initiative that Anuradha has taken, and asks her what interested her in the cause? She tells him that her ancestors are from Bangladesh, so when she saw him on the news talking about immigrants from Bangladesh and the waste-pickers, she also wanted to "do something" for them, therefore she thought of this event, this will not only make "Bharat Sundar" meaning beautiful, and it will also keep it "swacch," meaning clean, and help the waste-pickers.

He looks at her strangely, and after pausing for a while asks, "You are a Bangladeshi, right?"

She replies "My baba was... I was born and raised in Bangalore". Anuradha calls her father baba.

He asks her if she would be interested in acting in his film? She tries to conceal her excitement and says, "sure, why not, neki aur pooch pooch!" meaning you are doing something good and asking if you can do it?

DECEMBER 20, 2015

Prem Ratan has called Hero No. 1, Heroine No. 1, and Anuradha to his temporary office in Delhi for his film's story reading. The poster on the wall is a picture of two curved wooden staircases that lead to the same landing. And the wooden staircase is covered with a red velvet carpet. The staircase poster is on the wall opposite Anuradha, she keeps looking at it and remembering the many films that she may have seen similar wooden staircase in.

Prem Ratan tells them, "The three of you are garbage pickers in the film. Hero No. 1 and Anuradha are Bengali-speaking Muslims, and Heroine No. 1 is Bengali-speaking Hindu. The two communities are against Hero no. 1 and Heroine no. 1's relationship."

Anuradha asks Prem Ratan if she may suggest something.

Prem Ratan exchanges a look with Hero No. 1, and impatiently asks her, "what?"

She asks if her name in the film can be Mahjabeen Bano. Prem Ratan gives her a puzzled look?

.   .   .

Anuradha is staying at a 5-star hotel, which overlooks a 'gandi basti' meaning a dirty slum. She is looking out of her room window, down at the basti. She looks at her phone and dials a number "hello…"

"Ya Anu di, what happened?" Debu is sitting at the bar of the same hotel.

Anuradha asks Debu to call Sahyog Kendra and ask them if they can arrange a meeting for her, with the waste-pickers in any basti in Delhi?

. . . .

A workshop on Recognising Agency is going on at Indian Institute Centre. Priyanka, Midori, Shambhuji, Tahir Bhai, and a few others from Sahyog Kendra are sitting on chairs, with notepads and pens in hand. Vikram is writing in Hindi on the whiteboard

> 'Agency entails the separation of observation from evaluation.
> We need to clearly observe what we are seeing and hearing, without mixing in any evaluation.

Looks up at everyone, who are silently staring back at him. He turns around and continues writing

> Example:
> Agency - a person is forced to leave their country for safety and livelihood, without "legal" Documents.
>
> Evaluation - they are illegal immigrants and need
>
> to be sent back to their home country.
>
> Does the evaluation recognise the agency of the person?
> Does it support the person?
>
> Observation (without evaluation) - country is submerged in water, person needs food, water and shelter, person moves to neighbouring land, for safety and livelihood

Again he turns and looks at everyone, they nod in agreement. Shambhuji says that the police catch these people. Vikram asks him if he would like safety for them? He replies that they shouldn't catch them. Vikram asks him if they will get a promotion by catching them? He says that yes, they will have to prove themselves to their senior officers, no? Vikram continues prodding and what about the senior officers...

On the other side of the board is written:

Evaluations are to be based on observation:
Specific to:
Time
Context

Time - this area of land gets annually flooded
from June to September

Safety hazard - threat to survival'

Phone rings, Zublin tries to reduce the sound of the ring, by tightly holding the phone between his palms and hurries out to the hallway. The lighting is dim in the hallway, there is sunlight coming in through the concrete Jali, which is the term for a mesh in Hindi, at the end of the hallway. Zublin disrupts the beautiful baroque pattern of the jali reflection cast on the floor, as he moves away from the conference room. We can only hear his side of the conversation, he cups the phone in his hand and whispers softly into the speaker.

"Hello, Debuji, Yes? PAUSE. So nice. PAUSE.Oh, so nice! PAUSE. Bengali speaking Muslims, hmm ok, I will ask my sir and call you tomorrow. PAUSE. Ok, we will not tell she is actor PAUSE. Mahjabeen Bano? PAUSE. Oh! her film name. PAUSE. So she can get used to what? She doesn't know her name? PAUSE. Oh, her film's name, wow so nice!"

.   .   .

Vikram calls Guru Bhai who has established the Waste-pickers Welfare Foundation (WWF). His community approached Sahyog Kendra a few years back for their work and identity rights. He is educated in Hindi-medium, and he mentions that he was a 'Naxal,' but now chose to give that up and work with this community instead, also including that he can speak a little English.

"Ya Guru Bhai, how is everything?" — pauses "all right, then make me meet 'my blessing' someday?" — pauses — "there is a lady Anuradha, she wants to visit your 'Kamaal ki basti' to meet the waste pickers?" — pauses — "only if she visits there, will the reality of the place and the people, be reflected in her film, no!"-listening — "ya, it's at India Habitat, you're coming?"

.   .   .

EVENING
INDIA HABITAT CENTRE

Vikram has just given a talk on the Agency of Undocumented Immigrants. The talk was organised by a group 'Challo' to interlink the often conflicting sites of academic research and the lived community experiences, by facilitating interactive talks, seminars, and group discussions that are open to the public. Guru Bhai and many others are present.

A young boy stands and asks for the mic, "You're the most arrogant speaker I've ever heard!" The audience is agitated and murmurs begin.

Vikram responds, "Are you reacting to the views presented on undocumented immigrants entering the country?"

The young boy replies angrily, "No, you make it sound so simple."

Vikram guesses, "are you reacting to the fact that I didn't mention anything about how the process of recognising and supporting agency can be difficult for some people to apply?"

The young boy speaks loudly into the mic, "no, not some people-you!"

Vikram pauses for a second and responds, "so you're reacting to my not having said that the process can be difficult for me at times?"

The young boy calms down, "that's right."

Vikram asks for clarity, "would you like me to admit right now that this process can be a struggle for me to apply?"

The young boy thinks and responds, "yes."

Vikram responds, "Thank you, for your comment. Yes, this process is often difficult for me sometimes. How does that sound to you?"

The young boy seems calm and answers, "that sounds real. I have joined an NGO that works with immigrants, and my father is in the police. I am very conflicted when I hear his views. He believes that all immigrants are National threats and they should be sent back to their homes. But when I speak with the immigrants I realise that many of them are here only for livelihoods. It's like me choosing to work with the NGO even though my father keeps telling me to get a 'real' job. One that will earn the bread, but he doesn't realise that I'm getting much more from my work."

Guru Bhai raises his hand and the mic is passed to him, "You're not only getting bread, and you're also getting chickens muttons from working!" - the audience begins to laugh.

Vikram connecting with the young boy's needs, "I hear that you would like to continue working where you are for your need for learning?"

Young boy, "learning and reality. My father wants me to join a call centre!"

Vikram, "and you don't think you will find learning or reality in a call centre?"

Young boy, "what reality, TV is not working, fridge is not working, those are not reality." Audience laughter again.

Vikram requests, "can you say more about what is the reality for you?"

Young boy specifies, "these immigrants, they're real."

Vikram, "so the immigrants resonate with your need to support; for your need for learning?"

The young boy excitedly, "yes, yes, it makes me feel good!" The audience starts clapping.

Vikram smiles and says, "okay."

.   .   .

Guru Bhai, Vikram, and Zublin are having tea and biscoot, which is biscuit in Hindi, outside the discussion hall. Guru Bhai mentions, "That persons Anuradha coming tomorrow."

Vikram confirms, "Yes, she has said that she will tell the people in the basti that she is researching for her studies. As she doesn't want anyone to know that she is a filmstar, and get any publicity there. And remember to call her Bano. That's her name in the film, that's what she wants to be called by."

Guru Bhai responds, "Okay sir."

.   .   .

Zublin is taking a ride back with Vikram in his car, "It is nice to be telling that Anuradha is doing studies, that way media peoples won't come and look at the basti as if it is a museum.

Vikram driving, Oh yes, I agree, the basti is not a museum, unless, they want it to be, no?

Zublin confused, "why anyone wanting life to be museum sir? In your house, if peoples coming to photographing and leaving?

Do you think my need to be seen will be met?

Zublin further confused, but, but, okay sir, but they must take permission no? Is Guru Bhai asking basti people if Anuradha can go to their basti?

I guess not. Next time we have to request to go with him and speak with the basti people, about what they think, instead of just asking him for his permission, no? Zublin smiles, that is so nice idea, sir!

And thank you for the discussion Zublin.

Zublin feeling uncomfortable, shyly reacts, why sir thanking me, sir always speaking to you, giving me clarity.

It gave me clarity too!"

.   .   .

DECEMBER 22, 2015
SAHYOG KENDRA

Anuradha enters Sahyog Kendra's office room, Debu decides to remain on the balcony at the entrance. Anuradha sits in front of Vikram, at his desk. Zublin is also sitting on a chair beside Anuradha. Mimicking a Hindi Film actor Amol Palekar, "Hello saar!" The actor in the film changed the letter 'i' in the word 'sir' to the letter 'a' stressing on it and sounding it funnily pesky.

Vikram looking amused, "Please call me Vikram."

"Okay, and you please call me Bano for the next few weeks!" Both smile.

Vikram asks, "so you will be doing research for your film character in the basti?"

"Yes saar, I mean Vikram."

Vikram wonders and asks, "have you thought about what you would like to talk about when you meet them?"

"Not really, I just want to be able to listen to them and engage without any questions of my own. I want to understand what they are, how they think, how they speak, how they behave, how they live? So I thought that if I ask questions, they may think about their answers and react according to the questions. I don't want that. I want them to be themselves. And just spend time getting to know them. Just as regular humans. Not with my film on my mind. That's the only way I will be able to understand them for real I think?"

Vikram agrees and adds, "something like observation without evaluation?"

"Yeah, when I had done my course in acting in LA, I learned that to study or understand someone you have to drop your ideas of them, an actor doesn't have to copy the character they are playing, or mimic them, I want to find out the life of the character and what drives them, and draw those emotions from my own life experiences."

Zublin chimes in with inspiration in his eyes, "You are very thinking persons, how nice!"

Anuradha thinks a bit, then asks him if he said that she was a 'thinking' person because she mentioned the thing about actually listening?

Zublin responds, "yes, sar also tells us same thing."

Anuradha, trying to put the focus back on what needs of Zublin might be getting met, when he complimented her, "ah, so you appreciate it when people actually listen?..."

.   .   .

Self-resonance Diary. Note 2. I come across a timeline post-independence, of communal violence in India. Lives, safety, trust, everything lost in 1947 Jammu massacres, Pakistan's Operation Gibraltar, Moradabad riots, Nellie massacre, Gujarat riots, Hashimapur, 1990 genocide of Kashmiri Pandits, Punjab Killings, Operation Blue Star, Bombay riots, Pangal massacre, Bongal Kheda, First Kashmir war, Wandhama massacre, Amarnath pilgrimage massacre, Malegaon bombings, Jnaneshwari express derailment, 2000 Kashmir massacre, 2012 Assam violence, 2020 Delhi riots…. is your heart sinking Anuradha? Do you hear the voices of humans who want to be heard? Does your heart fill with grief and helplessness? Do you grieve about the humans that have died? Would you like to register a complaint with creation? Anuradha are you acknowledging structural and systemic power, and the importance of speaking about it. How it impacts the lives of every person living on our planet? I think of my worries about the larger world, about the price the earth's ecosystems are paying for us living out of relationship, out of responsibility, out of consciousness, without acknowledgment of our participation in our systems. I take a deep breath. My intestines are twisting. The muscles of my stomach ache from holding on, in remembered horror. My neck tightens, I stay with the reality of this violence. Being threatened with exclusion is too much for every individual. Anuradha are you feeling torn and drained of trust. You are visiting the homes of the humans both the Hindus and the Muslims tomorrow, for your need to support by listening to them, and support them how they need? Do you need rest now, so you can be in your body in health, and wake up and travel to all those humans who you are needing to support. So that you learn and grow. And create safer communities knowing that human beings start healing when they are heard. Good night Anuradha, I wish you a better sleep.

DECEMBER 25, 2015
AFTERNOON
GAZIPUR

'Door se dekha toh pahad dikh raha tha, paas jaake dekha toh koode ka landfill pada tha.' From far away, what looked like a hill, was a garbage landfill. The landfill spreads over 70 acres and is 50 meters high with 13 million tons of garbage. Vultures are hovering on top of the garbage landfill. A waste-picker is collecting garbage with his bare hands. He is wearing rubber slippers on his feet. Methane fumes are being emitted from the landfill and he has no mask on his face.

Kamaal ki basti is around a kilometer away from the landfill. The basti is enclosed by a dilapidated brick wall. Reddison Bleu, a worldwide upper upscale hotel, hovers on top of the basti. There is a taxi standing outside the Basti's entrance. Guru Bhai is sitting beside the taxi driver on one of the front seats. Debu is sitting behind him. And Anuradha next to him.

Debu tells Anuradha that he will check them in at Reddison Bleu and come to the basti. Anuradha tells him that she will be all right on her own. And that there is no need for him to hang around there for a free holiday, she asks him instead, to go to connect with the media in Bangladesh and let them know that she is starring in a Hindi feature film, "I need this news to spread so that Bollywood will know that I have finally arrived!" smiles.

Anuradha and Guru Bhai get out of the car and enter the basti. The waste-picker who was collecting garbage earlier from the top of the landfill, enters the basti behind them. Debu asks the driver to take him to Reddison Bleu.

.   .   .

Anuradha notices that there is waste piled up everywhere, she covers her mouth as lots of house flies are swarming around the waste. She dodges the dogs that are walking here and there. She notices the women separating waste from the waste piles, with their infants lying near them. She observes that they have used mud, bricks, stone, cardboard, and/or tin sheets to build their jhopadis which is the Hindi term for a hut or a shanty, and most of them have a mud stove called a Chulah in Hindi, outside the Jhopadi. Guru Bhai and Anuradha walk between the rows of Jhoppadis.

Guru Bhai excitedly throws his hands out, saying, "This is our Kamaal ki basti!" Anuradha glances at an area spread over a land approximately 2 kilometres in radius. They walk towards a ramshackle brick wall which is around four meters high. Guru Bhai informs Anuradha that the Hindus live on this side of the wall, and the Muslims live on the other side. Anuradha notices that the basti is unequally divided, 3 parts belonging to the Hindus and just 1 part to the Muslims, thinking perhaps that's because of the number of people belonging to the Hindu community may be higher than that of the Muslims. Guru Bhai, "come, I take you to other side."

.   .   .

Guru Bhai and Anuradha enter the Muslim side, Guru Bhai points to the fish shop. There is a big round blue coloured drum outside the fish shop. Anuradha peeps over, to find many eels lying inside the drum, which is filled with water. They continue walking, Anuradha looks down and walks carefully as the lanes are small with potholes filled with pools of stagnant water. Here she notices many women sitting with infants on their lap and chatting with each other, one woman is braiding a girl's hair, while 3-4 little boys are running around and playing.

Passing by a grocery shop Anuradha looks at an old man sitting and smoking his 'beedi' inside it, a song is playing from a transistor radio hanging at the entrance of the shop, Bagawaan humare hai meaning the lord is ours...

Guru Bhai and Anuradha reach an open area, which is behind the Muslim side of the basti. Anuradha asks Guru Bhai what this area is for? Guru Bhai informs her that this is the pooping ground, looking embarrassed. He notices few men who are casually standing around at a corner of the open ground talking, he immediately turns to go back, telling Anuradha that they are getting back to the Hindu side now. A pig passes by Anuradha, startling her, she quickly follows Guru Bhai as they walk back to the Hindu side.

They get back to the Hindu side. Guru Bhai looks relieved. He informs Anuradha that they started an informal school for the waste-pickers' children here, as one of the goals of the school was to meet and organise the parents of the children to build a community for the people facing similar issues. Anuradha later finds out from Zublin that Guru Bhai never pursued building the community, his efforts seem to revolve around the school only.

Anuradha is amazed to see how small the school is, there are two rooms, separated by a tin sheet partition. There are no lights or fan inside, the only light is the one entering from the broken concrete jali which means mesh window. A young lady is sitting on a chair and seated on a mat in front of her are 8-10 female and male children who maybe around 8-10 years old, except one little girl, who may be around 4 years old, sitting among them. The children are writing letters in English on their slates. They seem very happy to see Anuradha. Anuradha greets them, "Namaste!" They shout back hello to her.

One little boy has got a cut on his arm. Anuradha notices the cut and goes and squats beside him taking his arm in her hand. It is a deep cut. She asks how this happened?

The teacher replies that he went digging for pencil and paper in a pile of garbage when his arm got cut by a piece of broken glass.

Anuradha asks the teacher if they took him to a doctor?

The teacher hesitates and distractingly points up towards a wire-drawn across the room, on which some papers are hanging. Sunlight through the jali window is falling on the papers.

Anuradha gets up and takes a closer look, the children have drawn different things and coloured them. She is standing and looking down at the children, and asks them if they enjoy drawing? The children look up with keen eyes, and reply, "yes!"

Anuradha tells them, "Your drawings are very interesting." The children giggle and say thank you to her.

She heads towards the door, telling the children, "I will come again."

The children throwing their hands up in the air, "okay tata!" waving goodbye to her.

Anuradha smiles and waves back at them, "okay tata, bye-bye."

.   .   .

Anuradha and Guru Bhai are standing and chatting outside the school. She asks him, pointing to the Muslim side if there is a school on that side too? Guru Bhai tells her that children from there come here to study. She adds that it is useful that children from both sides study together. Guru Bhai proudly replies that they do not discriminate. Anuradha asks, "Then what is this wall doing here?"

Guru Bhai, "Arrey Banodi for safety purpose, you don't knowing this peoples are doing fights and robbing and all. Yesterday the neighbours came to complain."

Anuradha's throat tightens, and she clenches her teeth, thinking that there might have been a reason for them to do what they did, and how can he be sure that the neighbours are speaking the truth, and wants to tell him that, then decides against saying anything, as she doesn't want to get involved in this issue at the moment. There's a moment's silence, "Guru Bhai I want to meet Bengali speaking Muslim women."

He tells her that there is a basti called Chayapuri close by, he will take her there. She asks him why he needs to take her there, isn't this basti supposed to be of Bengali-speaking Muslims.

He looks frazzled, "No no."

"Then why did Vikram send me here?"

"We work with them, no, I will take you there."

.   .   .

Guru Bhai takes Anuradha towards two women. One of them is Jina, wearing jeans and a kurta which is an Indian garment worn by both women and men. Jina is sitting beside Chonchala on the ground and is sketching Chonchala's hand on her paper. Chonchala looks attractive to Anuradha who admires her Sari, an Indian dress, her bindi, a cosmetic decoration that Indians wear on the middle of their foreheads, and nose-pin and ear-loops. Chonchala is segregating waste.

Anuradha continues the conversation with Guru Bhai, asking him if there are no Bengali-speaking Muslims here?

Guru Bhai points at Jina and says, "Meet her, she is an artist."

Anuradha, "Hi, I'm Taa-Bano."

"Jina."

Anuradha asks Guru Bhai who the other lady is?

"Tell us your name?"

"Chonchala."

Guru Bhai's smartphone is ringing in his shirt's top pocket, he removes it and looks at it and moves away from there.

Jina looks at Anuradha, "Uff, these people, I am trying to make them understand that they have given birth to so many kids one after the other..." — nodding her head in disagreement, "but to make them understand..." — rolling her eyes up.

Anuradha "is not only difficult but impossible?!" while she sits beside Jina. Anuradha is also wondering why they have so many children, isn't it unhealthy for the woman, and also how can they afford to have so many kids.

The children are coming out of the schoolroom, and walking in the opposite direction from Anuradha. The little four-year-old girl can't take her eyes off Anuradha, she keeps waving her hand every time Anuradha looks at her and keeps tripping and falling, while her brother keeps picking her up. Anuradha looks at the little girl and smiles.

After a while, Anuradha who has been looking at Jina's sketch shifts her gaze to the apartments, and then she turns her head around and looks at the hotel and stares at it for a while. She gets transported to when she was standing by the window of a similar hotel and looking down at a similar basti. The only difference is that at that time she was on the other side, looking down upon the basti, and now she is on this side looking up at the hotel.

.   .   .

Guru Bhai is walking with a lady. She looks sturdy and walks with an air of confidence. She is wearing a bindi and comfortable 'chappals' slippers that are convenient to work in. Guru Bhai informs that she is the only woman in the basti who owns a cycle of her own. Other women do not venture out to collect or sell the garbage, but she does. She has a son who she calls Manoj. Her husband abandoned them long ago. She has been living in the basti for almost 8 years now.

"Banoji, meet her, she is Kiran Devi, or should I say that she is the Kiran Bedi of this place!" Anuradha thinks why Kiran Bedi of all the people, what with her politics, then the thought comes to her that well, she is a brave woman, so that's what he must be referring to.

Guru Bhai introduces Kiran Devi to Anuradha who turns her gaze from the hotel to Guru Bhai and Kiran Devi. Anuradha smiles at Kiran Devi and greets her, Kiran Devi gives a smile back to Anuradha. Guru Bhai informs Anuradha that his wife has cooked food for them at his place, and asks her if she is willing to go to his place? Anuradha asks him if he could bring the food here?

"Of course however you would like. I will go and get, if you have any trouble here, you tell her," pointing at Kiran Devi.

Anuradha signals Kiran Devi to sit beside her, Kiran Devi sits next to her.

Jina looks at Kiran Devi and says, "She looks sensible, why doesn't she make these people understand not to have so many children?" she looks at Chonchala and continues, "but she is instead telling me that the children help them with work!" - turning to Kiran Devi - "one must not make children work right?"

Kiran Devi asks her if she has children? Jina replies. Kiran Devi asks her if her son helps out with work at home?

Jina complains that she does ask him to help, "but you know today's kids!" rolling her eyes up, and then quickly adds, "but that work is different no, that's housework, and our kids don't get hurt at home? Here there are so many dangers in working…"

Kiran Devi, "that's the issue right?"

Jina looks nonplussed and looks at Anuradha, "Jina, I think she is talking about a safe workplace."

Jina agrees, "that's what I'm saying this place is dangerous for children to work."

"So would you stop them from working or would you create a safe workplace?" Kiran Devi asks.

"Bu… but this work… this, children should not be doing no? It's so dirty, it's garbage after all!" — shaking both her hands — "forget it, forget it, I don't want to get into a fight now. I don't think children should be cleaning garbage, and I don't want to talk about it right now."

Anuradha gives her an understanding smile thinking that if she hadn't read the report about manual scavenging and safety of the worker at Sahyog Kendra, perhaps she would've also been reacting like Jina. Anuradha then looks at Kiran Devi, "may I stay the night at your place?"

Jina looks at Anuradha with a part of her feeling shocked, surprised, curious, and scared, "will you be safe here?"

"I'm guessing that safety is a deep need for you right now?"

"Yes, yes safety is my concern, from that time I am saying this only."

"I hear you Jina, I do," wondering why she wouldn't be safe there, it is dirty for her, she will ask Debu to get her some fresh sheets from the hotel and if there is any danger Guru Bhai will let her know and she will go stay at the hotel.

.   .   .

AFTER A WHILE

Manoj and his friend are walking towards Kiran Devi. A Hindi film song is playing on his friends mobile '...kaam mera roz ka, char botal Vodka, kaam mera roz ka..' the lyrics translate as - having four bottles of vodka is a daily thing for me, Kiran Devi hears the lyrics of the song, gets up and charges to give the friend a whack. Friend puts the phone in his pocket and runs away. She holds Manoj's hand and screams at him, "I told you not to meet the boys from the other side?"

Manoj asks her for money? She pulls him by his ear, and asks where he was at all night? He doesn't reply. She lets go of his ear and holds on to him by his wrist and asks Anuradha, "Do you eat fish?" Anuradha nods a yes. Kiran Devi tells Manoj, "ae go to the other side and get fish and come," and lets go of his hand.

Manoj starts walking, Anuradha immediately gets up, and asks Kiran Devi, if she could go with him? Kiran Devi grabs and pulls Manoj back, "ae take her and," gives him a shake for his attention, "get her back with you and come."

Anuradha is trying to walk quickly behind Manoj, trying to keep pace with him. She asks him his name? She tells him that she wants to meet the Muslim ladies there, and asks if he knows them? Manoj doesn't reply to any of her questions.

They reach the fish shop. Three girls of ages 20-22 years are standing inside the shop. One of them sees Manoj and quips, "Here comes Kiran Devi's zero," and start giggling.

Manoj makes a face gesture at them asking them to shut up. They signal with their hand, asking him who the lady with him is? Manoj looks at Anuradha and asks her to come forward.

Anuradha introduces herself, "I am Bano, Mahjabeen Bano, I have come from Bangladesh to research," tries to think of a word for it in Hindi, "umm, to write a Kahani meaning story, on you."

The girls look at her shyly and giggle. One of them whose name is Zohrabai gets the fish from under the table and puts it in a plastic bag.

Anuradha asks what's your name?

"Nilofer."

Zohrabai, giving the bag of fish to Manoj, "Here take, this fish has come for Kiran Devi."

Manoj takes the bag and turns to leave.

Zohrabai calls out to him, "abbay, give the money?"

He turns around and holds one of his elbows by his other palm, and makes a snake sign with his free palm adding, "take it from Kiran Devi," and walks away from there.

Anuradha tells the girls that she will drop by later, and hurriedly follows Manoj. The girls nod their heads in understanding.

Anuradha follows Manoj walking past rows of rooms. Some men gathered in a circle, and are playing what looks like a card game called rummy. Some dogs are squabbling over a piece of roti, a type of flatbread.

Manoj and Anuradha continue walking and reach back to where Kiran Devi is, Manoj dumps the bag in Kiran devi's hand and runs away from there.

Debu is sitting on a chair, with an umbrella tied to the chair, lying beside him in a plastic bag is a bedspread, pillow, and duvet. He is talking on the phone, "Yes Sad di," pauses, "ya ya, Sadna that's what I am calling you no. Wha?" pauses "ya if Reddhisson is on your left, come straight, wait wait, I'm coming on the road.." he walks away with his phone.

He comes back with a girl, who is holding a photo-camera in her hand, he asks her to wait and goes inside Kiran Devi's room, Anuradha is tucking the fresh bedspread from the hotel on the bed, "That Sadna is here, that AD from your film."

Anuradha, "Ya coming."

They come out of the room. "Hi Sadhna"

"Hi ma'am"

"Please don't call me ma'am, you can call me An— Bano."

"It's okay ma'am, I'm used to calling you, ma'am. Ma'am please can you tell this Debu, he keeps calling me Sad di, can you tell him its Sadh ends with an h, he misses the 'h', it sounds so sad."

Anuradha smiles, "alright I'll tell him. Debu don't call her by half of her name, she doesn't enjoy it." Debu makes a 'what's the big deal' kind of a gesture and moves away from there. "So where do you want to take the photos?"

Sadhna points to a pile of garbage, "we'll start there."

Anuradha sits near a pile of garbage. Sadhna asks her to look at the garbage, acting as if she is thinking about Hero No. 1. Anuradha sits, Sadhna clicks photographs of Anuradha from different angles, moving 360 degrees around her.

A little crowd has gathered. They ask Debu what's going on, he tells them that Bano is researching for her studies, and for her research, they need her photos. He goes to Sadhna, "Sad di, hurry up people are getting curious."

Sadhna frowns at him and tells him that she is done.

.   .   .

Self-resonance Diary. Note 3. The permit system that Nehru introduced after the partition of 1947 comes to mind when you hear people protesting today-- speaking about secularism. I light a cigarette. Anxiety takes over me. Anuradha, do you have the fear of hurting people you need to care for? How can you care for everyone, being your authentic self? Was Nehru longing for equality, and didn't know of any other useful strategies to meet that need? Did he also have a need to be known? Are needs violent, or strategies to meet them are? Needs are universal and they just are. Was I present when it happened, will I be able to understand the complexities of that time just by reading history. Am I aware that history, media stories, research reports.. are all recorded by humans, and it is not free from evaluations? Whose story resonates with me more. Am I willing to turn my attention to the connection with feelings and needs? Ringing in my ear, some pain rises in my left ear. I join and press my lips, breathing is getting harder. Do I want a world where life is wonderful for all? Anuradha, what is your deepest longing, is it for every human to be seen and to be heard? I remember what Cheryl Richardson says, "People to start to heal the moment they feel heard." I hold my stomach down with both my hands, my throat hurts, and it has been hurting for weeks now. Anuradha, self-care, and self-empathy. Time pauses, sadness fills the space. I remember hearing that it is fair that those who chose to renounce Indian citizenship and move to Pakistan and then changed their minds and wanted to come back, be treated differently? Do you wonder that after partition, the choice to move to Pakistan or to stay back in India was tragic and may have been deeply difficult, as many who left their homes and country may have done so based on the fear that if they stay they may be treated as religious minorities in a divided country? It is not like today when we choose to leave our home and country and move to another country in pursuit of enriching opportunities. My head is spinning, needing to take a sip of water. My throat is overwhelmed with the memories of all the humans who are deployed to safeguard us, how they must live, some bear severe weather conditions. Many give up their lives for our safety, do you have a longing for safety for all. And you remember watching a documentary called The Long Shadow, which spoke about how humans were asked to celebrate those who died in the Great War, which was then called the First World War, after they realised there was going to be another war, to wash away their guilt of sending them to war and justify it by calling them, martyrs. Anuradha, are you feeling angry and disheartened? Do you also remember the soldiers' families who suffer their loss and are conditioned to feel proud? Anuradha is it disheartening that we would do this willingly to another human being? Everything seems to be moving fast. Are these your tragic expressions, for your need for safety for all. I press my left ear with two fingers. You want to say that in every riot, every war humans from both sides die. And you feel sad that we do not know of life-enriching strategies at this time. Would you enjoy peace and harmony with compassion? With awareness that in these times we cannot do away with borders as we would not know how else to safeguard ourselves. I choose to try and empathise with the ones I can for the moment and long for a world someday where security will mean security for all, even for our soldiers. I close my left ear with my palm and give it some loving care. Palm and ear get hot, feels comforting. Self-care and love to you Anuradha.

.   .   .

NIGHT

Anuradha and Kiran Devi are sitting outside Kiran Devi's room. Kiran Devi is making rice and fish. Kiran Devi has marinated the fish with red chilli powder, Haldi which is turmeric powder, and salt.

Anuradha is sitting beside her on the ground and speaking on the phone, "You stay at the hotel, no need to come and check anything," pauses "ya she is making fish and rice," pauses "don't worry I asked Guru Bhai, I'll be fine here."

Anuradha puts the phone on her lap and picks up the cigarette from her lap. She asks Kiran Devi to make her meet Nilofer, who she met at the fish shop in the evening. Kiran Devi nods an okay and dunks 4 pieces of Hilsa into a Kadai, a wok of hot mustard oil.

The fish is ready to be eaten. They finish eating and lie down beside each other, with their heads propped up over their folded arms.

Anuradha looks at Reddison Bleu and begins thinking that life for the people who live in such bastis is hard, comparing it to her own life. She recalls her day and thinks that Vikram, Zublin, Sadhna, Guru Bhai, Kiran Devi are all so interesting, and talking to them has been stimulating for her. She had imagined that they would be all serious, with grim faces all the time, talking in a soft barely audible serious tone. That wasn't how it was though. She makes a mental note to suggest Prem Ratan to take low angle shots, like Ozu, of the basti people who sit on the ground, as a tribute to the basti people being most connected with the ground!

Then she goes on to wonder that perhaps the ones who are richer than herself, might look down at her life and think that she has a hard life and they may feel sorry for her, with their notions of how her life should be, perhaps comparing it to theirs.

She recalls what she remembers Vikram saying, 'Researchers may have a different way of telling people's stories than how the people do. And sometimes when people hear the researcher's stories, it becomes their story,' - she lets out a sigh, feeling tired thinking about the many thoughts that are racing through her mind. She goes on to stare into the night sky, relaxes, and smiles thinking that she is grateful to be where she is at the moment.

Self-resonance Diary. Note 4. There is such joy to belong to a community that you resonate with. Anuradha, are you remembering the Nonviolent Communication intensive training in Germany? You were with 70 humans from all over the world. Many spoke different languages and still, you were connected by the living energy of needs within you. Are you agnostic just like Einstein, who believed in Baruch Spinoza's God, who reveals himself in the harmony of all that exists? Do you believe God to be the energy of needs that lives in the universe and inside us? Yes! And have you experienced the universe understanding the language of needs, when you send out your longings you receive back that energy? Yes, yes, yes! I remember a friend of mine who is religious, he told me that when he asked his God for a gift, he received an idol of that God from a friend. To me, he sent out a longing for maybe his need for abundance and received that. The same friend resonates with a group called RSS, my friend sounds angry to me, and when I connect with him I hear frustration and pain below that anger and longing for needs same as mine. I read that RSS encourages cultural expression, yes a strategy for communication. Communication connects us all. Anuradha, when you hear that they do not want to "take shit" from Muslims any longer, and they have been attacked for so long, that now it is time for them to defend themselves and kill the "terrorists/termites," do these words come down as blows on you? You hear the tragic expression of unmet needs. I breathe slowly and close my eyes. What is it within me that would want me to kill someone? What feelings do the words self-defence and terrorists bring up in you - fear, insecurity, pinning for safety, security, and the word justice comes up for you. You ask your friend if he needs justice, and you notice your friend melt a bit, just as you sense that melting within yourself. He thanks you for listening to him, you both look into each other's eyes, tears well up. Is your heart going to explode with the energy that you are sharing? Can we find it within us to empathise with those even we do not agree with? Loud sigh, it is so very hard, and when it happens, it is what makes me feel truly alive! Anuradha, do you wish to share your learning -- you do not have to agree to understand? And you Anuradha, you do it because you have a need to empathise, for your own need for harmony, safety. Yes, yes the more I empathise the safer I feel! Anuradha, do you wonder if this is enough for the absence of the desire to do harm. Connection and aliveness to you Anuradha!

DECEMBER 26, 2015
MORNING

Swarms of flies hover over a pile of garbage, besides which Anuradha is sitting with Chonchala who is pointing at different piles of waste, "This is file."

"You'll call paper, file?"

Chonchala continues, "this is paper," - pointing at the newspaper stack - "this is Pepsi," - pointing at empty tin cans of Coke, Pepsi, Thumbs Up, etc. - "this is plastic katte," bands used for tying cardboard cartons, "'botal,'" empty glass bottles.

Anuradha exclaims that they have given such interesting names for different categories of waste.

Kiran Devi appears with Nilofer, who seems like she is maybe in her early twenties, and has an infant hanging on her hips.

Anuradha looks at her and says, "Oh hello, remember we met yesterday?"

Nilofer nods and smiles.

"Is this your child?"

Nilofer replies, "Yes."

Anuradha asks her the child's name?

"Khushi"

Anuradha, "oh she looks so happy, just like her name Khushi," and pinches the baby's cheek. She asks Nilofer to speak in Bengali. Nilofer says that she can't speak in Bengali, as she is from Bihar. Anuradha wonders why Prem Ratan thinks all these waste pickers are Bengali?

. . .

Guru Bhai is walking towards Anuradha with a man, who is smiling and seems like he walks with spring under his feet.

"Good marning Banoji! You alright in the night?"

"Oh, a very good morning to you too Guru Bhai! Yes, I slept like a baby."

"Good, good," wiping his sweaty forehead, "look here who I have got, this is Mahatoji, he is boss man of here."

Anuradha smiles at Mahatoji and asks, "Are you the big boss of this place?"

Mahatoji is continuously smiling.

Anuradha asks him if he knows what is written on his t-shirt? He tells her that he doesn't know how to read? Hesitating, she looks at Guru Bhai and wonders if she should tell Mahatoji what is written on his t-shirt, then goes ahead and says it, "I'm smiling because they haven't found the dead bodies yet!" She looks nervously at Mahatoji for his reaction? Mahatoji bursts into laughter. Anuradha is relieved and starts laughing with him. Guru Bhai hesitates and then joins them in laughing.

Guru Bhai informs Anuradha that Mahatoji was the first person to come here, ten years back. She asks why he chose to come here?

Mahatoji tells her that there was no one else here before he arrived, "I came here first and this place became mine!"

Guru Bhai tells her that they earn money by selling garbage. Adding that, "This is not just garbage, it is gold, there is kooda meaning garbage, mafia. But sarkar the government, calling this peoples chor thieves."

She asks, "Why do they call them thieves?"

Mahatoji says, "They make us do the work and they call us thieves, and they do not give us the license to do the work."

Tring tringg.

Anuradha asks, "Why not?"

Guru Bhai takes out his phone from his pocket, looks at it, and walks away with Mahatoji following behind him. Anuradha looks at them wondering and needing to know why they don't have a permit to do this work, and then how are they still doing it?

. . .

Anuradha is sitting and chatting with Kiran Devi. Debu walks towards them with Zublin who has come along to meet Anuradha.
"Hello, Anuradha!"

Anuradha widens her eyes and gives Zublin a stare, smiling.

"Whose Anuradha?" — nodding her head, wondering how she can remind him to call her Bano and not Anuradha in the basti — "Bano, Bano," — Zublin gives a blank look — "my name is Bano, Zooobleen!"

"Haaan, how nice!" laughs embarrassed, for forgetting that she requested to be called Bano.

Kiran Devi looks at Zublin and Anuradha confused.

"Kiran Devi this is Zublin from Sahyog Kendra."

"Namaste!" — to Kiran Devi - "So Anu u u bb, Bano are you talking to all peoples here?"

Anuradha laughs, "Yes, I have got to meet many people here. I feel really happy. And I keep asking Guru Bhai to make me meet with Bengali women, and I'm starting to understand that they are mostly from Odisha and other parts of India, and can't speak Bengali. Then why do people assume that they are Bengalis from Bangladesh?"

"Who told you they are Bangladeshis?"

"My film director Prem Ratan"

"How does he thinks they are Bangladeshi peoples?"

"They have done recce," Zublin gives a blank look, "recce means they have come and checked many bastis. And read on the internet about waste pickers, I think that's how they may have come to this assumption."

"Government is wanting to push back Bangladeshi Muslims daily, so they are saying all these people are coming from there, and hiding in such bastis. Then they hire Mukhbirs,"

"Who?" Anuradha interrupts, "Mukhbir means?"

"Mukhbirs like CID"

Anuradha, "yeah like Daya and Pradyuman?"

Zublin laughs, "yes CIDs, you are so funny, so nice. They are hearing peoples wearing skull caps and white pyjama talk in Bengali and saying they are Bangladeshi and illegally pushing them back."

"Whaaaat? Why? I speak Bengali, and I am an," — whispering — "Indian!"

Zublin continues, "that Firoza in our office, she is speaking Bengali, and she is Muslim but from India only. She get very angry when peoples are thinking she is Bangladeshi." — takes a pause — "till when you will be meeting peoples?"

"Another 2-3 days. Then I'm going to meet my parents before the film shoot begins."

"Oh wow, how nice!"

Anuradha asks Kiran Devi to go to the toilet with her. Debu asks her to go to the hotel with him to use the loo there, as he is anyway going to drop Zublin to the road.

Anuradha remembers that the loo area is on the Muslim side, and she is eager to go there again. So she tells Debu that she wants to experience going to the loo in the open for once in her life! And walks with Kiran Devi to the other side. Debu and Zublin head to the road.

. . .

Anuradha has squatted, while Kiran Devi is standing and holding her dupatta around Anuradha. Anuradha can see Kiran Devi's feet, and hear her shoo away the pigs, who wait for any potty droppings along the way. Anuradha gets up and asks Kiran Devi, "Paani ka nal kaha hai?" where is the water tap.

Kiran Devi says, "Not there."

Anuradha looks puzzled and wonders how they clean themselves? She asks Kiran Devi, "There's no water supplied here?"

"No."

"Why?"

. . .

They get back to the Hindu side, Guru Bhai and Mahatoji are standing and talking to each other. Guru Bhai is telling Mahatoji that they need to get 3 ID cards made. Anuradha takes Guru Bhai aside, where a broken unwanted cane basket that is lying on the roof of a room, casts a shadow of a meshed pattern on her face. "I want to go to the hotel."

"All is well?" he asks her if everything is okay.

She tells him that there are no water taps here, and she needs to freshen up, so she needs to go to the hotel, shower, and get back. She asks Guru Bhai why there are no water taps here?

Guru Bhai, "arre, we trying to get water, their promise on paper water is there," — pauses — "what to do Banoji very low caste here," — whispers — "their wanting to keep them smell"

"What? But why," she feels very confused, "why do they want them to remain smelling?"

Guru bhai sighs, "the smell is their identity, and there being other difficult things for them, dogs are also getting smell and bitting them."

Anuradha looking alarmed, "that sounds cruel."

Guru bhai smiles and says, "what I say Anuji, he only taking care," - looking up at the sky.

Anuradha rolls her eyes in her mind, then thinks just like she believes in the energy of the universe, he believes that there is a God up there, she responds, "that's your faith that there is someone up there taking care of things, you believe that things will get safer and fair?"

Guru bhai, "yas Anuji, Gaad God is great!"

Anuradha smiles, "okay."

. . .

Anuradha can see a humongous bulldozer charging toward her, person driving the bulldozer resembles director Prem Ratan, she is lying on the ground and wants to run but can't move, Prem Ratan is speaking with the DOP and pointing a finger at Anuradha, "this girl is from Bangalore and she can't speak proper Hindi," - someone is whispering in her ears, "the police have brought a bulldozer," with blurry eyes she turns her head and squints and tries to focus, someone grabs her, and drags her out of her room. A constable is holding her by her elbow. She is trying to comprehend what's going on.

Cops have arrived in the basti, it is around 10:00 pm, they have dragged her out of Kiran Devi's room.

Kiran devi, Manoj and a few other basti people are standing around. A discarded broken concrete jali lying around casts a pattern with shadows on Kiran devi's room wall.

The constable whispers into Anuradha's ear, "Do you have ten thousand rupees?"

Anuradha tries to push him away, and break herself free, and is unable to. She looks at Kiran devi, who looks back at her ashamed. Anuradha asks the constable, "What's going on?" and asks him to let go of her.

The head constable comes close, and gives her a tight slap on the cheek, "Shut up you bloody Bangladeshi thief," and asks the constable to take her away with them.

Anuradha is shaken up, and dumbfounded, she can't speak a word. Anuradha and the constables leave.

Kiran devi is tightly holding Manoj's wrist, she looks at him, "Tune mukhbari ki na?" she guesses that he must've told on her, to the cops for money? - she shakes him up and asks him to speak. She slaps her head and says, "What will I tell Guru bhai now?" and starts beating up Manoj, while Manoj keeps smiling wryly.

. . .

The cops are taking Anuradha to a detention centre. She is sitting in a police van surrounded by male-cops, feeling scared and extremely unsafe and trembling with fear. And wondering why and where they are taking her? After a while she looks at the person who slapped her, and wonders why he slapped her, she wants to scream with anger and fear, she wants to grab something and hit everyone in the van to somehow break herself free and get out of this situation that she is stuck in, her breathing becomes faster, her throat starts hurting, she closes her eyes and tries to focus on her thoughts trying to connect with his needs, looking inside herself - what is it within me.. that would make me shout at someone, calling them a thief, no he called me a "Bangladeshi thief".. How did he know I'm Bangladeshi, someone would've told him that and why?.. Where could these people be taking me.. If they think I'm Bangladeshi, do they know I was at the basti for research? If they know I'm doing research why would that make them arrest me? And if they don't know I'm doing research, ya he said "Bangladeshi thief" ahhh maybe he thinks I'm a waste-picker, that's why he called me a thief maybe.. And maybe someone did mukhbari, spied on me for money, like Guru bhai mentioned, as I told the basti people that I am a Bangladeshi researcher, damn.. Feeling curious she continues guessing, hmm so this man thinks I am a Bangladeshi, a waste-picker and a thief, now how would I think if I am this man - I am bound in duty to catch such persons, and this person is struggling to be let go of me?… Anuradha, are you feeling rage and when you slap this person, are you experiencing satisfaction in this moment out of a kind of cruelty? A soft response, yes. The use of force to frighten another into doing what I want them to do, so that I can have access to care for myself.

. . .

DETENTION CENTRE
SHAHAZADA BAGH
NEAR SHASTRI NAGAR METRO STATION

It is enclosed by a high wall, with a main entrance gate, which is not locked. Once you enter there is a rectangular open ground. On the other side of the ground, is a building, from end to end of the ground. There are two entrances to the building, one is to the left, and one in the middle. The one in the middle is locked. And there is an armed guard sleeping on a chair, right outside that door. On the entrance door is a sign reading ren basera night shelter, a translucent white tape is pasted on the sign. Perhaps to hide it or to rename it.

The constables take Anuradha to the left entrance, which is the office area. There is a door to the right of the office, they take her through that door to a corridor that joins the room where the detainees are kept at. There are two chairs lying outside the door in the corridor. The constables, keeping a watch, outside the door have opened the door, and are inside the room. There are around 40, 6 ft x 3 ft cloth mats lying on the floor, arranged in two rows, opposite each other, for the detainees. There is a wall on the opposite side of the door. And 5 windows on the right wall, and 4 windows and the other entrance door on the left, facing the ground and the main entrance gate. The constables stay on the first floor. There are only 2 toilets, one for the staff and the other for both female and male detainees.

15 MINUTES EARLIER

Lalchand Saddar Ali goes up shivering with cold to a constable and asks for a chaddar blanket. The constable laughs loudly and asks Lalchand, "you want a blanket?"

Lalchand nods a yes, constable points behind Lalchand, Lalchand turns around to look, "here take a kick," giving him a kick on his butt, and laughs out loud.

Lalchand tumbles forward, constable goes and twists his ears and takes him to the left corner near the corridor door, and tries several times to make Lalchand squat. Lalchand makes his body loose, so each time the constable pushes Lalchand downward, Lalchand falls sloppily to the ground. Then another constable joins in, they try together several times, then the constable kicks Lalchand hard on his butt again.

Lalchand springs up in pain, and squats down like a cock, crowing, "cookadoo coooo," in pain.

Ameena Begum is about to burst, she needs to pee and cannot hold it in any longer, "I need to go to the bathroom." Ameena must be just in her early thirties, and hardships of life show on her face, through her well-defined features and deep facial lines, making her look much older than her age.

"No need to go to any bathroom vathroom, why do you people eat and drink so much that you have to keep going to the toilet?" Constable replies, pushing her towards the mats.

A Constable enters with Anuradha.

The constable who pushed Ameena goes up to her, picks her by her arm, and takes her to the corner where Lalchand is squatting, and asks her to do her job there. He is about to pull her saree up, and Ameena pushes him, and Anuradha rushes to Ameena and covers her with her own saree "pallu". When Ameena is done, the constable points at the mats, and asks them to move over to the mats. Ameena goes to her sleeping mat, Anuradha goes and sits down on the empty mat beside her.

One of the constables calls out to Lalchand, "you cock," all constables laugh, "c'mon lick the chaddar of pee now," the constables break into uncontrollable laughter, one of them goes and drags Lalchand and presses his face over the urine.

The constables leave the room and lock the door from outside. Anuradha is lying on her mat facing away from Ameena. She is unable to sleep, she is feeling cold. She turns and faces Ameena, whispering, "Why have they kept us here?"

"To send us to Bangladesh."

"Really! Is this the detention room… I wanted to go to Bangladesh from here."

Ameena says, "I want to go back to Bangladesh," - and farts.

Anuradha laughs. Ameena gives her a puzzled look. "Why do you want to go to Bangladesh?"

"I am from there, they got me here and married in Rajasthan. I went to fetch water, where I met a truck driver, he told me that if I get married to him, he will bring me to Dilli. So I came here to Dilli with him. I used to live in Chayapuri, the police raided the place, and got us here," — pauses — "Why do you want to go to Bangladesh?"

Anuradha wonders quietly asking herself — to research for part in Prem Ratan's film? — wondering if it was all right for her to stay at the waste-pickers basti at Gazipur to research for her film, her own need to learn would've been met, and what about the community's needs, would any of their needs be met by her research or film?

. . .

DECEMBER 27, 2015
03:00 am

It is dark inside the detention room, all the lights are out. The corridor door opens. Sound of whispers enter the room, "Abbay will you stop weeping like a whore."

Light from the bulb in the corridor slowly tries to creep inside the room. Moonlight falls on the dark floor, on the boy that the two constables throw inside the room. The boy looks alarmed, he has a fresh wound below his left eye.

The Constables exit the room and lock the door behind them. One of them crashes into one of the chairs, he is still weeping and trying to wipe the bloodstains from his hands with a handkerchief.

Weeping Constable, "This blood stain isn't getting wiped off."

Constable 2, "What blood stain?"

Weeping Constable, "even the entire water of the Yamuna river cannot wash these stains away.. in fact, the blood on my hands will make the entire Yamuna red."

Constable 2, "abbay madarchod, motherfucker, firstly there is no blood, and secondly, if you go to wash your hands in the Yamuna, Yamuna won't become red, maybe your hands will get burnt."

Weeping Constable looks dazed and continues crying.

Constable 1, "abbay fucker, have you gone mad or what?"
- gives him a tight slap.

. . .

MORNING

The young boy who was thrown inside the room the night before is sitting with his arms wrapped around his legs in the corner. Four detainees are cleaning the windows on the right wall. Ameena is mopping the floor. Lalchand, Anuradha, and Anwar are cleaning the windows on the left wall.

Anuradha whispers to Lalchand, "When did they bring you here?"

Lalchand whispers back, "It has been two months," — pausing — "if only I had ten thousand... well, anyway, as the constables say, now I can go and visit and enjoy a new country, for free!"

Anuradha gives him a puzzled look and smiles. Lalchand has been to school till the 4th grade in Calcutta. And he has papers to show that he can vote in Calcutta.

Anuradha looks at Anwar Miya and awkwardly moves to the window next to Anwar's. Anwar Miya is around fifty years of age, he has been illegally deported twice in the past. Shadow of the iron jali on the window envelopes Anwar's face.

Anuradha whispers, "Dada in Bengali for elder brother, when did you come here?"

Anwar Miya smiles at her and replies, "I have been brought here 3 times," takes a pause, "I even have my school certificates and my land ownership papers," pauses again, "but what can be done," — sighs.

Anuradha suggests that there is an NGO called Sahyog Kendra, if they all get together and go there, perhaps something could come out of it for them? He doesn't reply. She wonders why he remained quiet on the chance of getting support. She is about to ask him why when he responds, "we have tried everything, now I think we should just go sit in front of the parliament and beg them for our lives, what other choice do we have," — takes the bucket of water and moves away from her.

. . .

AFTERNOON

It is afternoon, and dark inside the room. The lights are off, some sunlight sneaks onto the floor. Anuradha is sitting beside Ameena. Lalchand and Anwar are also sitting around. The young beaten up boy is also sitting in the corner, with his head hanging low. Some detainees are standing pressed at the window facing the ground. Four people are walking on the ground towards the left entrance of the building.

"Who are you?" "Why have you come here?" "Who have you come for?" Anuradha and Ameena look up at the detainees standing across them, who are looking outside asking these questions.

"..kaha se gori ankhon main pyaar leke, Dilli sheher ka saara meena bazaar leke.." a Hindi film song blares from a loudspeaker outside the detention room. One young boy gets up and starts dancing. The other detainees also turn around. Anuradha and Lalchand begin clapping.

The door opens and one constable enters, everyone freezes, "Aye you," the constable is looking at Anuradha, "come."

Anuradha becomes numb, and is unable to move, the constable goes and picks her by her shoulder, and tugs at her arm. She manages to move and walks trippingly with the constable.

Anuradha is standing at the entrance of the office. She can see the officer who slapped her is sitting at a table, with a passport in his hand, speaking with four people whose backs are turned toward her.

Officer, "She is Indian?!"

One of the four people hands the officer a paper saying, "it is the letter from the FRRO."

The officer takes a look at it, and then looks up and sees Anuradha standing at the door, "come here, please."

All four people turn around, Anuradha is relieved to see Vikram, Zublin, Debu, and Guru Bhai and tears start rolling down her cheeks and she starts sobbing uncontrollably.

"take your passport and go from here, please."

Debu gets up and goes over to Anuradha, she holds his hand tightly, Vikram takes her passport from the officer. The five of them exit the office.

In the compound, just before exiting the main gate, Anuradha hears someone calling out to her, "Anuradha,

Anuradha.." She turns around, everyone from the ground floor room is pressing themselves to the windows, Ameena is waving goodbye to her.

Anuradha waves back with tears in her eyes. They are still inside the compound behind the closed gate. She asks Debu to take her back home.

Vikram goes to her, "If you become this way, then how will you do your work? How will you make your film?"

Anuradha looks at him and says, "But I am not making the film, Prem Ra…" — she doesn't finish what she was about to say.

Vikram asks her to take rest and, "come and meet with me tomorrow, before you leave back to Dhaka," — exiting the main gate of the detention centre.

. . .

DECEMBER 28, 2015
MORNING

Anuradha enters Sahyog Kendra, Vikram looks up at Anuradha and asks her to sit, "How are you doing?"

"Rested," her mind can't stop thinking of the detainees, she's wondering what will happen to them.

Vikram asks her what she plans to do after she returns to Dhaka?

"I can't work in these types of films anymore. I can't find meaning in them for me."

Vikram asks her if she would be interested in making her film about her experience?

She looks at him wondering, "I haven't thought about what I'm going to do yet. For now, I'm going to meet Prem Ratan to tell him that I am dropping out of his film and then to meet Kiran Devi to say bye to her before I fly out at night…"

. . .

Debu is standing on the balcony smoking a cigarette with Zublin. Anuradha and Vikram also join them.

Anuradha lights a cigarette, Vikram asks her why she doesn't want to go to the newsroom debate, "after all, these discussions are happening after news of you being detained came to light right?"

Anuradha, "I am happy that this discussion is going to happen, but I need to go back and reset my mind a bit. Right now with the thought of all the people who are going to be there, I feel overwhelmed thinking about it."

Vikram, "I understand. Take rest and get back, we will be waiting for you here."

. . .

AFTERNOON

Anuradha has come to meet Prem Ratan. The stairway film poster has now been adorned with a golden frame, hanging on the ceiling is a crystal chandelier hanging low from the ceiling. The reflection of the crystals fall on the stairway poster

ANURADHA

I am grateful to have had the chance to work in your film. I stayed with the waste pickers for my part in the film, and I got detained. PAUSE. I realised that I have a need to contribute to the community, by working with them. And I will be unable to continue working in your film.

PREM RATAN

What? Are you saying that you do not want to act in my film?

ANURADHA

I have had many different experiences these past few days. And I have a need to be heard.

PREM RATAN

You want your ideas in my film? I'm the director of this film, I knew I shouldn't have taken any of your suggestions. You actors are so hopeless. Why can't you actors just keep quiet and do what you are asked to do? Why don't you go make your film if you want to be heard?! LAUGHS. You'll get to know how hard it is to make a film!

ANURADHA

I do not want my ideas in your film, I am saying that I do not want to act in your film any longer. PAUSES. I understand this is hard for you.

PREM RATAN

Nothing is hard for me - RAISING HIS VOICE - you know how many friends I have in the industry? And you obviously know who I am? I can make 30 such films in a year! Just go from here, I do not want to ever see you again.

ANURADHA

Raising her voice to be heard and match intensity - do you need commitment?

PREM RATAN

Enough! Just leave. I am not dependent on you. I can make a call right now, and there will be 100 other actors waiting to work in my film. I don't need you.

Anuradha rises and starts walking towards the door. Debu also gets up and goes behind her.

PREM RATAN

Anuji, you can forget about your Bollywood dreams...

Anuradha holding the doorknob, turns her face around, acknowledges Prem Ratan, and turns back around and leaves with Debu walking behind her. Prem Ratan dials a number from his phone.

Heroine No. 2?

. . .

EVENING

Kiran Devi is sitting outside her room, combing her hair while chewing tobacco. When she sees Anuradha she immediately gets up and goes to her and holds her by her hands, "Banodi."

"Not Bano, my real name is…" they start walking towards Kiran Devi's room. Guru Bhai and Debu follow them.

30 MINUTES LATER

Anuradha and Kiran Devi are sitting on the bed, near the entrance of the room which is around 5 ft x 10 ft. A tin sheet is used as a partition in between. Debu is standing beside Guru Bhai and notices the TV, heater, and a cooler that is kept at the end of the room, facing the entrance. A single bulb throws some light into the room. Sunlight entering through the Jalli window falls on Anuradha's face, casting a pattern with light and shadow.

"Manoj ran away that night itself."

On hearing this, Anuradha mourns, "regrets, this would have never happened if I hadn't come here."

"The police would've caught him someday. It is good that this happened now and he ran away. Now the builders are also going to bulldoze our basti. We will be on the roads soon,"— bends her head, and holds it with the palm of her right hand, shaking her head slowly.

Anuradha asks, Guru Bhai, "why don't you do something?"

Guru Bhai replies, "our lawyers are getting the stay order!"

After a while, they are standing at the door. Anuradha hugs Kiran Devi. Kiran Devi awkwardly touches her back.

. . .

DECEMBER 29, 2015

The daily newspaper 'Chimes of India' carries the following headline:

BANGLADESHI ACTOR KICKED OUT OF PREM RATAN'S FILM HEROIN NO. 2 REPLACES HER

Next to this, on the side column:

INCOMPETENT LAWYERS COULDN'T SAVE KAMAAL KI BASTI!

. . .

EVENING
NEWSROOM/NEWS CHANNEL INDIA

After the news of a Bangladeshi actor, who was illegally detained reaches the media. Vikram along with the leader of a political party, and a human rights activist have been invited by a news channel to discuss 'Labour Migration and Citizenship' on their show — 'Debate Ek Asha' meaning: Debate A Hope.

The journalist introduces the panel, "On the panel tonight are Shakuntala Misra representing All Government and Political parties (AGPP), Vikram Azad from Sahyog Kendra which provides consultancy services to mass organisations and communities, and Sanjay Gogoi who is a human rights activist from Assam.

Illegal immigrants are coming from outside our country and becoming a law, order, and security problem, they have changed the demography of Assam, and they are snatching land and jobs from our Deshvasis. AGPP has decided to completely seal the Indo-Bangla border by 2018. Our high court has ordered that these immigrants be deported back to their countries under the Foreigners Act - where the arrested persons have to prove that they are not illegal.

So tell us what measures do these illegal immigrants take to prove that they are not illegal?"

Vikram asks, "Could you use the term 'undocumented or Informal' instead of illegal to address the migrants?"

Journalist replies, "if they are undocumented, then they are illegal infiltrators no?"

Vikram responds, "it is also true that large numbers of migrants perform informal labour without or with false documents - because they have no other way of securing work and also because the Indian system breeds upon and enables corruption. In fact, their illegal status gives further leverage for victimisation at the hands of contractors, police, etc, because, in India's rank-ordered society, every social weakness serves to augment exploitative arrangements - a kind of negative 'social capital'. Waste pickers children are the worst off, and often sexually victimised."

Shakuntala chimes in, "okay so you agreeing no this people are illegal! Swearing on holy cow mother, if I'm saying the lies, you cut my head no, this infiltrators who are terrorists, they belong all to one religion."

Journalist affirms, "terrorists do not belong to any religion."

Sanjay agrees, "Terrorists do not have a religion but they do belong to one religion only."

Journalist rolls his eyes, "moving on, AGPP is planning to seal the Indo-Bangladesh border by 2018, what's the panel's opinion on it?"

Vikram guesses, "it could be one of the thousand strategies for security?"

Journalist questions, "if only sealing the border will ensure security?"

Sanjay quickly adds, "yes, it will stop these infiltrators from coming inside our country. These infiltrators are taking over our country's land."

Shakuntala agrees, "if you provide land and food to these vulnerable infiltrators, and give them weapons, they spread terrorism."
Journalist retorts, "why and who is giving vulnerable migrants weapons with land and food?"

Shakuntala sounding confused, "what I don't know all this, I know this land is our's motherland, and we protect it"

Sanjay replies, "the government is taking away land from indigenous tribes and the farmers, in the name of development, development of the rich. Public projects are actually designed for private profits."

Journalist adding a fact to Sanjay's point, "according to the Ministry of Tribal Affairs (MTA) nearly 85 lakh tribals were displaced until 1990 on account of large developmental projects." - looking at Shakuntala - "do you know who this land is sold to?"

"It is sold to big industrialists and to infiltrators," replies Sanjay.

Vikram asks, "shouldn't we stop and ask why the government who sells land to these people, are now interested in deporting them?"

Shakuntala repeats, "what you are saying, those we want to deport, those are infiltrators."

Vikram, "who is allowing them inside the country? And for what?"

Sanjay places blame and reacts, "this AGPP is doing all this for votes and profits."

Shakuntala remarks unwittingly, "what you are saying, we are not letting peoples come to India okay! We are making border wall with these profits for your people's safety only."

Vikram asks, "won't universal opportunities for all school pupils and integration of informal labourers with universal rights in the worldwide economic activity cost us less than building a wall?"

Shakuntala retorts, "how it will cost lesser if there are extra persons to take care of."

Vikram slows down and reflects back to Shakuntala what he heard her say, "so you're saying that the economy is crashing, there is a lack of education and jobs because extra people are entering the country?"

Shakuntala, "yes, that is why we are making the wall to keep out this terrorists."

Vikram, "so I'm hearing that you think all undocumented immigrants are terrorists?"

Shakuntala, "yes they crossing border illegally."

Vikram, "so would you like to offer people from the regions where there are violence, poverty, and persecution refugee status?"

Shakuntala, "yes our Hindu minority people which getting persecooted in outside countries, they can come to India"

Journalist sounding restless, "Shakuntala how are Muslim Bangladeshis detected for deportation?"

She replies sharply that they catch the Muslims who speak in Bengali...

Journalist bangs his palm on his desk furiously and retorts, "many Bengali-speaking people are Indians and they can be Muslims and Hindus and how can you say that only those who are celebrating Durga Ashtami are welcome?"

Shakuntala justifies, "all Bengalis celebrate Durga Ashtami, not only the Hindus."

Sanjay agrees with her, "this argument is irrational. The infiltrators have changed the culture and demography of Assam and now they are spreading to the rest of the country as well."

Journalist quips, "let's not talk about cultural alteration Mr. Gogoi, your son is working in the US."

Sanjay, "that is different. I sent my son because there is so much unrest in Assam and I wanted my son to go to a safer place with better opportunities, with a legal work visa."

Vikram remarks, "he was able to apply for work, get the job, and a legal work visa, I'm wondering why the undocumented immigrants are unable to apply for the jobs they do like waste-picking from their countries, get the job, and a legal work permit and identity before entering the country?"

Sanjay feeling extremely irritable, "it is all informal work no, how they will apply from there."

Journalist asks, "Why is it informal?"

Shakuntala replies, "Too many peoples, so work becomes less."

Vikram informs, "that's because the employment problem is structural, this means in recent years employment became de-linked from growth, economic expansion became led by its services sector, and when farmworkers exited agriculture in large numbers and manufacturing did not expand, these workers were absorbed into construction and services, both sectors dominated by low-paying, low-skilled and informal jobs."

Sanjay adds, "the informal economy has been described as 'the economy not covered by official data on registered enterprises' and therefore not registered for taxation and/or regulation by the state. The fact that it is not officially regulated does not imply a complete absence of regulation. There are many unofficial means of regulation. Quite often activities that do not possess registration and legal sanction get denoted as informal or 'underground'. This practice results in the official erasure of the economic value of the goods and services produced therein. It also serves the purpose of masking the over-exploitation and socially levered extortion to which the most unprotected and vulnerable members of the working class are subjected.

Shakuntala, "now you are putting wrong blame on us. You saying we are robbers or what?"

Journalist, "then what? Immigrants want jobs, your citizens want jobs, who is going to give them jobs, your register? Your wall?" Instead why you don't provide immigrants a chance to a fair trial for which first the definition of citizenship should include the concept of livelihood, the flow of migrants should be regulated by issuing permits to those who desire to work in the country as per international convention on the protection of the rights of all migrant workers and members of their families, and by issuing them ID cards through labour exchange. Provide a system of accountability of authorities entrusted with the tasks of detecting, detaining, and deporting unwanted immigrants. Foreigners act to transfer the burden of proof on to arresting authority, so the people arrested are "innocent until proven guilty." And detention based on the human rights approach?

. . .

DECEMBER 29, 2015
BANGLADESH

Anuradha mutes the TV, she is sitting in her drawing-room with three of her friends - Nimrit, Nayan and Shamuli, who are visiting her from Bangalore.

Everyone's sitting silently lost in their thoughts, suddenly Nimrit speaks, "AIUDF party chief Bhadruddin Ajmal has opened a floodgate for these immigrants, and Rohingyas too, and then the communist took them to Kerala even."

Anuradha replies, "it is not Muslims who are the threat. It is the government that shows them as threats. So the government doesn't have to do any work. And just blame and name people as outsiders. Fear of immigrants, to blame and cover-up for the work they never intend on doing."

Nimrit continues what he was saying adding that the communists took them to Kerala too.

Anuradha guesses that he doesn't enjoy Rohingyas in the country because they are a threat to the country?

Nimrit responds, "This mindset is a threat, Rohingyas need food, books, contraceptives, it is the Wahabi mindset."

Anuradha continues to engage, "so you think resources are limited and they are going to those who are not Indians?"

Nimrit continues with a burning to be heard, "a completely warped version of what Islam is, there's enough for everyone, but because there's enough you don't feed it to the virus. There will be a demographic change and it's soon happened in many states, fuelled by vote bank politics, if your religion asks you to hate and change, and prays for you to be at peace something is fundamentally wrong. It's like antibiotics. My land is being taken by Rohingya settlements, my fault that I and my family worked hard for it, 2-3 Jholla Walas can talk all they want in the garb of Human Rights... But where is mine? My mistake was to make a decent living for myself and to keep my family secure."

Nayan "dude it's normal liberal stuff, people who don't allow their own countries to develop because of their inherent religious and cultural shortcomings then want to go to countries that have developed and then bomb, criminalise and destroy them."

Shamuli looks at Nimrit, "look at Bangalore how it has changed ya, so many people from outside have come, and the traffic is getting worse day by day because of them. Anuradha our city has become dirty and it's suffocating to live there, it's not the same as it used to be."

Nayan adds that the AGPP is making the fact that many are unable to speak Kannada in Bangalore, a linguistic issue claiming that Kannada, is endangered."

Anuradha adds, "I remember growing up in Bangalore there was a ban on movies of any other language besides Kannada being shown in theatres."

Nayan informs, "The IT industry centered in Bangalore depends on there being a steady supply of English-knowing graduates. And condoning English would be to cut off one's nose to spite one's face. Bangalore,

Karnataka's capital and largest city, is one where languages other than Kannada seem to predominate, such that Kannadigas are needing to use English or another language just to communicate in their state capital! And there is the resentment felt by Kannadigas that speakers of other languages, such as Tamil and Marathi, get away with ignoring the official language, while in their states they ignore linguistic minorities such as Kannada speakers. A sense of unfairness seems to predominate, crying out for redress."

Anuradha responds, "yes I understand this, and I do wish I was taught Kannada and Hindi in school better, I struggled to connect in Hindi with the waste-picker community in Delhi and I struggle to connect in Kannada with the locals in Bangalore. I regret that deeply."

"No point telling her all this, she has become one of those righteous people living with those waste-pickers and meeting those Jholla-gangs in Delhi, now she is supporting these Bangladeshis.." Nimrit says looking at Anuradha for a response.

"Whether it's Muslims, Hindus, police, AGPP I have a deep need to care for all humans," responds Anuradha.

"I agree, but somewhere in that realm, you need to voice out against this shit.," says Nimrit.

Anuradha asks, what shit?

Nimrit nods his head and says, "If you still don't see it... I'm sorry, you're just blinded by the agenda and fake narrative floated around...And by not voicing out Wahabi

Islamic heads make it a Muslim issue than a Hindu issue... How right or wrong do you feel you are being?"

Anuradha empathises, "I hear you have a need to care for Hindus, I do too."

Nimrit looks surprised, "really, ever visited the Kashmiri Pandit refugee camp? It's just that they were chased out of their home in 1990... for the heinous crime of being Hindu."

Anuradha, "that's sad?"

Nimrit goes on, "no it's a shame, how pathetic of them being Hindu right? I mean why care about them? For you Muslim camps must be a priority?"

Anuradha responds, "all humans are an equal priority?"

Nimrit smirks, "gets all the funding," - loudly, spelling it out - "LIBERALLY!"

Anuradha matches Nimrit's tone, "if that's the case, I agree that's sad, it should be equal?"

Nimrit shaking with anger, "ya, but you won't raise your voice for the Kashmiri pandits, it doesn't fit the line or narrative of your NGO's and Jholla gang!"

Anuradha smiles, "are you a 100% sure about that?"

Nimrit bangs his fists on the table and gets up and looks at Nayan and Shamuli, "I'm just going out for a bit."

Nayan gets up, Shamuli replies, "let him be, I think he needs some space alone." Nayan sits back. Nimrit steps out.

"I should've just listened to him instead of telling him what I thought," Anuradha speaks almost to herself. Whisper from within, "I also need equality and inclusion," - breathes - self-empathises with her needs for inclusion and equality. Chooses to empathise with herself then with others to connect.

Shamuli reassures her, "forget it na, he keeps talking about all this saying that these immigrants and all are making India dirty, why people can't live in their own country and all, when he is living in the US himself. As if we keep India very clean!"

Anuradha guesses that it sounds like Shamuli would like a clean place to live in? Shamuli says that she wants a better lifestyle and quality of life. Anuradha continues checking that perhaps she thinks that this may not be possible in India? Shamuli thinks and says maybe not. To which Anuradha asks if it's sad and maybe even painful sometimes for her. Shamuli says no. Anuradha asks her to say more. Shamuli says that she has a good life, Anuradha guesses adding a safe, clean place to stay, a job, and friends like her? - smiling. Shamuli says yup. Anuradha asks if she feels grateful for that. Shamuli says yes, Anuradha asks if she has hope that things can improve? Shamuli says nope, with age it will all go downhill.

Anuradha realises something and says, "ah, you're concerned about health?"

Shamuli gives clarity that she is thinking about age rather than health. Anuradha tells her that she has heard Shamuli appreciate how Anuradha looks like she is in her mid-twenties, even though she is 41. Shamuli exclaims, exactly! "thanks Anuradha, it is really nice meeting you after such a long time."

Anuradha asks, "what was nice?"

Shamuli wonders and says that it is nice, like talking to her. Anuradha smiles and asks if she enjoys connecting with friends?

Shamuli responds, "yes and I appreciate how you don't react to things you may not agree with."

A part of Anuradha feels uneasy, "I try very hard not to react and sometimes, only sometimes I manage to empathise," - a part of her feeling encouraged, "would you enjoy pausing and responding instead of immediately reacting?"

Shamuli says that she would surely like that, "but it is so difficult yaar, I don't know how you do it?"

To which Anuradha suggests, "practice, practice, practice!"

Nimrit enters seeming calm, everyone looks at each other, Anuradha thinks and then asks Nimrit if he would like to talk? Nimrit nods a yes. Anuradha shares her intention with him, telling him that she doesn't want to attack him, and even if she may not agree with something she truly wants to understand and she is willing to hear him fully till he is complete. Nimrit says that he is also needing safety and that includes for all, period. Anuradha agrees.

Nimrit continues to inform her that the Hindu population in Pak was at 22% today it's at 2-3%. Anuradha says okay listening to him. Nimrit continues, Hindus are blocked in all aspects of social life, they are not allowed in civil services and the army. They don't get an education, admission to top universities.

Anuradha guesses that's unfair? Nimrit says, absolutely unfair, comparing that with the quotas the Muslim and Christians get in India, and how Hindus struggle through it to get into good colleges. And adds that if one googles Hindu girls in Pak, you will read about the horrendous acts against Hindu girls, as young as 9 years old or less, abducted, converted and married off, that's the Wahabist mindset. He asks Anuradha to watch Pushpendra Kulshetra to see a rather educated breakdown of many issues about Pakistan and Islamic extremism and the Islamic state that is creeping into our system, adding that Islam is not wrong, and sharing that the Quran is brilliant and scientific, it's the wrong interpretations that are venomous, and the lesser educated are perfect brain-fields for these seeds of misinformation? Anuradha agrees that people can be brainwashed.

Nimrit says that his wife and he want to have a baby, but then they discuss if they will be able to provide a safe life for their child, and if yes only then they will have a child, not like the Wahabi mindset where they want to keep multiplying. He says that having children is fulfilling, but making children for an innate religious reason, that's a disease! It's sick if it's based on religion, whichever religion — Hindu, Muslim, Christian...

Anuradha clarifies, "it's sick if it's not out of being responsible for the life you bring into the world?"
Nimrit responds, "absolutely!"

Anuradha asks if he feels frustrated when people procreate because their religion asks them to without thinking about the consequence of that life? Nimrit agrees, saying that the reason is that they are going to be creating a life that will only learn from their environment. Anuradha checks if he would like reality, growth, and maybe learning? Nimrit adds, earning is learning, and earning is not necessarily money, money is not the only thing that makes one rich. Anuradha guesses if he is thinking about meaning, purpose, and experiences? Nimrit adds relations, larger purpose, impact, experience, and says yes. Anuradha responds that she understands.

Nimrit feeling frustrated suddenly adds no one understands, for the first time in ages I can be who I am, and openly say I go to the temple every Tuesday, and don't eat meat on Tuesdays, without feeling embarrassed, thanks to this government who supports and encourages us to follow our Hindu beliefs openly. He is breathing heavily. Anuradha reassures him saying that she understands it's frustrating when people laugh at something you believe in. He exclaims yes! As if what I support is somehow lesser, and I am less. That is what I don't want. I want to express myself openly, without feeling scared. I'm not telling people what to believe in or who to support or mocking them, why can't they just let me be me! He pauses continuing to breathe heavily. Anuradha softly keeping her gaze on his eyes empathises, "it's frustrating even disheartening when people who think differently from you try and convince you to agree with them, and when you don't agree with them they mock you, calling you names?" Nimrit replies ya calling us Bhakts, what are they then also bhakts of what they believe in. Anuradha asks, "like what they believe in and support is superior and you are shallow and inferior. And the holier than thou attitude must be annoying?" Nimrit responds, "yes, yes very annoying, that's what is saddening, its.." - looks for words. Anuradha guesses, "it's sad because this is what is separating people from each other?" Yes, Nimrit replies, his body relaxes, and his breathing becomes slow and calm again. Anuradha continues looking at him. He stays silent. Both perhaps feeling safe and not needing to verbally attack each other.

Nayan asks Anuradha what she thinks, Anuradha says that she understands and agrees that everyone has a right to be themselves openly as long as they are not harming anyone else, she adds a real example of a friend of hers who got married, her friend told Anuradha that her husband wanted to take her friend to Europe to make her meet his friends. She was so scared to go because her English wasn't good, and she thought that the Europeans would make fun of her. Anuradha told her so what if they make fun, even the friend used to make fun of Anuradha because she couldn't speak Hindi very well. The friend says sorry. Anuradha is about to tell her not to feel sorry, and reassure her, then she empathises with her friend and realises that her friend was feeling very scared of embarrassment, so she says, it can be embarrassing right? Her friend agrees. Then Anuradha informs her friend that most Europeans speak their local language, unlike India, they do not look down upon you for not knowing "proper" English. Her friend's English may be better than many of the Europeans. Her friend told Anuradha that she felt super happy to hear that, and was feeling relieved.

Nimrit adds that even though it is wrong that people make fun of him, he does not wish to do the same back to them. Anuradha replies that she fully agrees, and asks if he believes that justice means justice for all? Nimrit says that he is tired of being blamed and shamed, he too doesn't want violence, he is just scared of the Wahabi mindset, that the vulnerable in India can get influenced and brainwashed by it. Which is a threat to the survival of our religion? Anuradha thinks and reflects so your fear is your religion and ways are at threat you need to save it from other violent religions?

Nimrit softly says, "no, we need to stand up for ourselves by way of enacting laws which protect our rights and make this country truly secular and not secular. For pseudo-seculars and armchair intellects, even talking about protecting Hindus is harmful. We should not worry about them. However, we should not resort to violence unless the opposite party does it."

Anuradha reflects what she heard back to him, "I hear that you would enjoy justice, and I need to let you know that I am feeling extremely sad because I think that you are referring to me when you talk about armchair intellects, and I would like to understand for safety."

Nimrit looks at her for a few moments, "I love you Anuradha, you are a dear friend and I will never harm you, never."

. . .

Self-resonance Diary. Note 5. I visited my therapist this morning. I told her that I have a fear of ghosts, when I am home alone, I often lay awake thinking that if I sleep a ghost will appear. She asked me what will happen if a ghost appears? I said that the ghost will take a pillow and strangle me. My face has tightened, my eyes hurt, there is much pain in my jaw and throat. I remember my mother mentioned that when I was an infant, my brother who was only two years old, took a pillow and tried to strangle me. There! That is my fear - I will not be able to breathe, all the dots connect - claustrophobia, fainting in underground metros and crowded spaces, head and ears feel hot, I can't breathe. Fear is fear and you just have to connect with it, hear it. Ask it what it needs. The Muslims fear they are minorities and their lives are threatened, the Hindus fear that if they don't maintain their majority status, they will be wiped. I hear that fear. Anuradha, would you enjoy holding all fears with care. Being gentle with it. Sending out a longing for ease and love in the universe. I hear a memory of pain that is shouting, saying that the Muslims invaded our country, I have a need to hear that pain, to be gentle with it. Are you needing justice, belonging, maybe safety, a longing to be heard, and to be seen? I long for justice for all, where every human is restored to their human self. Is it possible for this way of living? I send out a longing for justice and harmony for all, out out and out to the universe.

. . .

This story continues to unfold.

AUTHOR'S CLOSING THOUGHTS

Marshall B Rosenberg's quote comes to my mind, and I would like to share that with you, "If I use empathy to liberate people to be less depressed, to get along better with their family, and at the same time not inspire them to use their energy to rapidly transform systems in the world, then I am part of the problem. I am essentially calming people down, making them happier to live in the systems as they are, and I am using empathy as a narcotic."

Next time you feel frustrated and even maybe disheartened, about the broken world you live in, and want others to understand, try self-empathy (connect with your own needs) and then check with yourself if you are willing to move from separation to togetherness? You don't have to feel connected to or even like the other person/s, you just need to know that togetherness will be self-serving and life-serving for all (not just the "good" guys).

Talking to my friends who have different political ideologies of the Right, Left and/or Centre, something changed — I changed, I experienced an expansion in my openness to accept differences in strategies, as I realised that we all have the same needs.

So for me, it is no longer any other choice, its nonviolent collaborative togetherness or nonexistence. Systemic change cannot happen only on an individual level, we have to each start now where we are and think of ways of applying it in the systems that we are part of or will be willing to be part of, according to our capacities. And like what I also hear an NVC facilitator Miki Kashtan say, I do not know if this is the way that will work, as I cannot know about what has not yet happened, I cannot imagine any other way at this moment to be part of change. I don't claim of being able to live in NVC consciousness all the time, it's hard, as I have millions of years of DNA to change, and at this time, I know that I choose to keep trying. As I hope that someday maybe 1, 2, 3, 4, or more generations from now, humans would have created a world where there is the absence and the need to do harm and we speak the truth with love, which is the basis of all nonviolence.

Warmly and with love,
Menaka Neotia, New Delhi, June 2020

Acknowledgments

My deepest gratitude to the following without whose willingness to connect and dialogue with me, this story would not have been possible:

Nikhil for supporting me, by clearly understanding the requirement for the cover, and communicating the same to Vikas Thakur, the illustrator. I feel so happy with the book cover. This and for his presence in my life. My friend Cma who saw the cover and title said what it meant to her, "all the people around the women are telling her — hear me, hear me." I am enjoying the clarity of communication through the illustration.

Mom for always loving me, and trying to understand me. Chachiji, Chachaji. Papa and Naniji thanks for believing in me and loving me, and my need to matter is met because of your presence in my life! Kiara and Aloo for taking an interest in knowing about the Bengali speaking humans. Adi, when I gave up, I heard you tell me, that I am capable of doing much more in life, and for asking me to take responsibility for my choices. Roops for wishing the best for me and loving me always. Shaun and Bobs for your love and acceptance. Roops and a few others, whose names I cannot recall at this time, for suggesting I made the film into this book. Amzu you were willing to give me all the money you had in your piggy bank, to make the film to let people know about the plight of the waste-pickers. Kiu, Aloo, Amzu, Deetu, Manu, and Duggu my loves. Guddu didi, Chinu didi I wish that you get all that you need - love, support, to be seen, to be heard. My mother and father's families that I feel belonging to — Kiran Bhabhi, Sunil

Bhaiya, Suman Bhaiya, Saroj Bhabhi, Badi Buaji, Tikki, Abhishek, Rahul, Sunita, and everyone.

Thorat, Bipin da, Devesh, Madhur, and Sumit I am grateful that you reached out to me and discussed your views with me. I see this as your need to connect. I received understanding, learning, connection, and safety. And I no longer feel attacked even verbally and need to defend myself and/or attack you. Ranjana Massi, Koti. Ayan, grateful for the discussions you have with me and the information I receive. Sukrut I needed to care for myself and you, and I wish that you find the support that you need.

Marshall, I am not sure I would ever enjoy living if I hadn't got to learn the language of life that you shared. Sudha I start healing when I am heard by you. I love you. Biraj I learn to love from you, Manasi I receive acceptance from you, Pravas I feel seen by your presence for me, George for hearing me, Tithya, Pali, Vivek, Annie, Priti, Deepankar, Prachi and every human in the NVC Delhi practice group I feel happiest to be part of our community and empowered. Tiwari Ji and the space and snacks! I feel lucky and grateful to have Sudha, her listening, support, love, and guidance in my life which is healing and life-enriching for me. Grateful to Anja for the NVC IIT experience in Germany, I saw that humans can be different, have conflicts and if we are willing we can live together nonviolently. I now see how we are all connected in the flow of life! Also gratitude to all the translators who made all our differences in the way we speak work for us all. Pancakes for your support, community, joy, and love. Kanini and Mel I enjoyed sharing room space with you, I felt so comfortable and at home with you. Stefi for listening and sharing and adding joy, Anneli I miss your reassuring hugs, Jenny for sharing breakfast time with me, Isa for the sharing on the bus, Mubarik for connecting with me by your memories of Bollywood, Ido for your caring feedback and for suggesting Grammarly to me, Kathleen for your time and I always remember the love in your eyes each time I looked at you. And everyone I met at the IIT I am grateful for your presence in my life. Jan and Irmtraud I receive learning and support. Annett I remembered the time when we "saw and heard each other" and cried and laughed both together, I will never forget how I felt! Georgios for the meaningful session on the power of circles. And the entire global NVC community. Thank you Ranjitha for connecting with me. Also Anja and the people who made our stay warm and comfortable with their hospitality at the IIT, I miss the German cakes, the fresh, healthy, and delicious food and the lake at Schieferpark. Grateful for the presence of Miki Kashtan and the work that she is doing. Sarah Peyton, I learn from your daily self-resonance, so much that I was able to express myself authentically, with care for all. I feel inspired and I have deep gratitude for your presence in my life. Marta for your willingness to support my learning and be part of the Mediate Your Life course at Weimar!

Dunu Roy your experience can teach a lot if we want to learn. I met my need for support and to be seen by working with you. I feel grateful to have you in my life. Mukesh da for your encouragement, Pankaj for the help with budgeting, Ranjan & Ajay for your inputs, Priyanka without your encouragement the visit to the Ren Basera turned into a detention center would not have been possible and all at Hazards Centre.

Dilip Simeon is one of the people I know, who choose to understand, engage, and connect nonviolently. Your guidance expanded my mind to delve deeper and has made this book turn out the way it is. Deep gratitude to Kartikay for staying interested and keeping the civil society meetings with Dilip Simeon going on.
Bali Bhai and all at the real Kamaal ki basti for always making me feel welcome among them, and sharing their lives with me.

The Lee Strasberg Theatre and Film Institute where I met some of the best teachers. David for having faith in me and making me realise that I can act. Sasha Krane for showing me the connection between cinematography and emotions. And every teacher didn't have to "break" me and with mutual trust and respect, I was able to perform in surprising ways there! Dhingra for being excited about this story and trying. Niren for offering support. Joseph Mathew for remembering me and writing me the best recco. Seema Bhabhi, you wanted to contribute to my studies in acting. Kavya Iyer for encouraging me to act. Shambhu for reading and appreciating. Anand dada. Sheila Didi for understanding me, and without whose support Strasberg would've remained a dream. Varun for your inputs. Peace da and Noopur for taking interest in listening to the story and your inputs. Ron for your valuable inputs and excitement about the project, you are a part of this work. Rtg, Flatter. Nish, I feel cared for and supported. Ritu without you, I would have never been able to gain all that I did at Strasberg. Aditi, Sagar, Sudha massi, Appu uncle,

Dips, Biju, and all the melodious ones in Dubai. Bina Chachi & Vrijesh Uncle for making me feel at home. Nikki for your love. Sreejith for encouraging me to go do the Strasberg course. Ashraf & Jaimini I learned a lot from you. Peace da, you may have noticed, your inputs made the story authentic. Pranati for trying to connect me with Netflix. Sheikoo and Mo for hearing the story and your keenness to contribute music to it. L, Doc, Amin for your interest in what I do, I feel encouraged. Rips I felt heard chatting with you in New York. Shefali, Ady, Mallu, Teju, Ashish, Shyni, Juhi, Andy, Navroze for your care and support through one of the hardest times in my life. Diksha. Manik Atya for the laddoo. Ketu, Ashwini didi, Bhashkar. Ajji for your inclusion. Ajoba.

Upama for your book writing tips and your feedback, I hadn't thought about the difference in writing dialogues for a film script and a novella before you mentioned it to me. Deboo deeply grateful for your support with editing that were able to give, I received care and clarity from your feedback. Sivapriya, I've heard that when we speak with someone like they matter, they start feeling like they do. That's how I feel when you speak with me. Bishal talking to you was helpful for me to act. Subhs for chatting with me. Sohini for suggesting I include citations. Girsh, Mahesh mere do anmol ratan. Akshat for your inputs. Ayushi, Yesashwini, Ishaani, Akash, Sneha, Manjima, Padmapriya for your love, Kaavya regrets that I couldn't be the friend you needed at that time, Sindhu for your love and care, Robin, Mynaks, Ajeya, Aastha and Rachna I miss you at work, Sarah I remember our fun times and discussions, Sudha I will always remember the caring hug you gave me and your encouragement, Tarini, Simran, Aditi, Nemisha you shared the meaning of the word "justice" as you understand it with me - that met my longing to understand and receive justice, Madhurima, Noori, Shruti, Pali I feel considered by your care, Padmapriya, Ela, Sonu Unkal, Mobes, Sindhuri, Priya, Mrinal, Rahul, Shweta, Loveleen, Shrey, Manan, Niharika, Vaibhav, Ardra, Amrutha, Ranjini, Abhimanyu, Ram sir, Deepakx2, Ivjyot for listening and discussing, Shibani, Abhinav for connecting with me, Mushtakji for your encouragement, Preeti, and all at Sahapedia.

Pranjal my friend and brother, who I discuss science, relationships, and life with! Meena Atya my need for acceptance and love is met in your presence. Anja, thanks for listening and for your inputs and suggesting the name "Kamaal ki basti." Suman for being a friend indeed. Mitu for our discussions and new perspectives. Babu for sharing your ideas with me and encouraging me to make this into a film. Vidsy for your pieces of advice. Lisa, Niru for your love and support. Harish uncle I am always interested in the discussions you bring up with me, it meets my need for stimulation. And Poonam aunty I wrote the bit inspired by Macbeth in my book after you involved me in the seminar on Shakespear organised by you, that has enriched the understanding of the perpetrator's dilemma in the book.

Thorat I appreciate your caring and support. Sneha for your love. Papaji for your love. Ramesh Uncle, Sheru, Tara grateful for your sharing and listening to me, Badi Anju, Sudu dada, Nikhil Rao, Neelam Gheewala, Shibu, Adu, Sagar, Anshul Joshi, H, Shobha Aunty I enjoy watching old

Hindi film songs with you. Carreen aunty, Lambi, Divya, Shivani, Nidhs I enjoy and look forward to our conversations, Sanyasis for being excited and supportive, and for willing to chat and connect, PTis grateful for the conversations, Olis miss you, Happis, Robi da Tandon. MPB my science buddy, Jazz who is willing to connect on the level of feelings and needs, Anoushka for your love, Vikas, and Partho for discussing various things with me which deepens my understanding, Rwits for your care and celebrations. JnS, Ira gratitude for your inclusion during the lockdown. Pran Jal, Surang, Apu, Neha< Avinash, and all at Newsclick. Osbin for your recognition of my practice of NVC, Tari, Guppu for our many bhais's.

Nehs my sister from another mother. Usha aunty -- your love and care for my family, Raju uncle for sharing your music with me, Chandani Bhabhi for your love, Nikki bhaiya. Ahiku and Arya my darlings. Akila aunty and Mammad uncle for your love and for seeing "love" in my eyes. Shaggu Appa, Zene Appa, Zo I miss all the fun we had together when we were children. Ayesha I miss you. Suba. Mithu, Shwetambari, Kavi, Sanjay, Ravi, Talls. Devi, I miss loafing with Roops and you in Cunningham road. Rimma for connecting with me. Mahendro my bro from another mo. Eishu and Miryu. Nanju. Nayana for coming back into my life. Amu I miss your parents -- their care for me. Dhruv. And all my friends in Bangalore. I miss my childhood city's weather, trees and gardens, and my dosa, sambar, and chutney from there among so many other things.

Gratitude to Diksha for proof-reading, and I appreciate that she told me she was doing it for the love of the language, she found time and when she was busy or needing rest she took a break for balance. I didn't need to follow up with her as she was proofreading for her own need to contribute and for stimulation, and her way of working met my need for trust, ease, and support!

Everyone and those I forget to mention, thank you for being part of the flow of making this happen.

REFERENCES, TRANSLATIONS AND SUGGESTED FURTHER READING

*Note: Most of the conversations and experiences mentioned in the story are taken from the author's real life and/or are inspired by real events/people and have been mentioned below.

AUTHOR'S PREFACE AND CLOSING THOUGHTS
1. Book and Youtube Video by Miki Kashtan:
    a. Reweaving the Human Fabric
    b. Exiting the Either/Or Trap - Beyond Consensus vs. Command and Control
2. Marshall B Rosenberg - quotes from the book - Nonviolent Communication - A Language of Life

SELF-RESONANCE - DIARY ENTRIES
2. SARAH PEYTON - SELF-RESONANCE ON FACEBOOK; more on - www.empathybrain.com
    a. In simple language and easy-to-follow exercises, Your Resonant Self synthesises the latest discoveries in brain science, trauma treatment, and the power of empathy into an effective healing method that literally rewires our brain and restores our capacity for self-love and well-being.
3. The Long Shadow - documentary resented by Cambridge University historian David Reynolds.
4. Dyad Meditation practise sessions by Annett Zupke, inspired by Robert Gonzales.
5. Language of Life - Marshall B Rosenberg
6. CNVC facilitator - Sudha Shankar
7. Religious and philosophical views of Albert Einstein - Isaacson, Walter (2008). Einstein: His Life and Universe. New York: Simon and Schuster, p. 390.
8. When Anuradha mentions visiting homes of those affected by the riots she is referring to the 2020 Delhi Riots, author is visiting homes under the "EmpathyForDelhi Project", held under EnCompassion, a

peace-building and conflict transformation firm that will work with NVC Empathy-based processes to listen and focus for long-term trust-building across communal lines.

9. Violence, riots, exodus, massacres:

    a. Maulana Azad - India Wins Freedom published in 1988
    b. Timeline of Kashmir Conflict - wikipedia
    c. Painful disclosures - Special Report News - Issue Date: Nov 15, 1988
    d. THE FORGOTTEN MASSACRE THAT IGNITED KASHMIR DISPUTE - RIFAT FAREED - www.aljazeera.com
    e. 1980 Moradabad riots - Wikipedia
    f. Nellie Massacre - Assam: India's Ethnic Cleansing - Restless Beings - www.restlessbeings.org
    g. 1985 Gujarat Riots - From Gandhi to violence: Ahmedabad's 1985 riots in historical perspective - Spodek Howard
    h. Hashimpura massacre - Wikipedia
    i. 1990 EXODUS DAY - www.epw.in
    j. PUNJAB KILLINGS - "Sikhs attack India trains, killing 126". Chicago Sun-Times - www.en.wikipedia.org
    k. Bombay riots - 1992-93 - Engineer, Asghar Ali (7 May 2012). "The Mumbai riots in historic context". The Hindu. "Full Srikrishna report: Chapter 1". Sabrang Communications.
    l. 1993 Pangal massacre - How mob justice in Manipur was given a communal tone By Chitra Ahanthem
    m. 1998 Wandhama Massacre - wikipedia
    n. Gujarat Files: Anatomy of a cover up - Rana Ayyub
    o. 2000 Amarnath pilgrimage massacre - wikipedia

p. 2006 Malegaon bombings -   How the state makes Muslims pay for Hindutva terror - Arun Ferreira And Vernon Gonsalves

q. Jnaneshwari Express derailment - Hard rain falling on death of Chandrasekharan - www.dilipsimeon.blogspot.com

r. 2020 Delhi riots - wikipedia

s. Bongal Kheda - Wikipedia

t. 2012 Assam Violence - wikipedia

FILM, THEATRE, NEWS/MEDIA, LITERATURE/POETRY CONTEXT IN THE NOVELLA:

1. The scene number 1844 mentioned during the filming of Prem Ratans film is the birth year of Chandranath Basu - Wikipedia - Basu coined the term Hindutva, which was popularised by Savarkar.

2. Read about what sounding the clap board means here - Why Do They Click That Board Thing Before Filming A Movie Scene?

3. The character Prem Ratan is inspired by
    a. "Sanjay Leela Bhansali - Wikipedia."
    b. "Bal Thackeray's cartoons | IndiaToday."

4. The parts in the book where Prem Ratan is speaking with anyone is deliberately presented in a film script manner, as he sounds like he always has a script ready, out of which he is saying his dialogues.

5. Lyrics of the song in Prem Ratan's film are inspired from the song "Kai baar yoon bhi dekha hai ye jo man ki seema rekha hai ...." from the film Rajnigandha.
    a. Kai baar yun bhi tum dekho, yeh kachra nahin, mera dil hai.. Means Sometimes take a look at this garbage
    b. and realise that this is not garbage, it is my heart..

6. The character called Heroin No. 2 is loosely Inspired by "Priyanka Chopra - Wikipedia."

7. The song that Anuradha is humming in the beginning of the story in her kitchen is from the song "Kaise Din Beete - Lata Mangeshkar - YouTube."

8. The author learnt about light in cinema at her training at Lee Strasberg, and she decided darkness follows Bano and light falls on Anuradha due to their social status - Anuradha belonging to the upper-middle class and privileged and Bano belonging to the lower working class and victimised.

9. When Bano is trying to sit on the swing and is unable to, that incident in the book is inspired by the scene with Utpal Dutt and Dina Pathak from the Hindi feature film titled "Gol Maal - Wikipedia." Gol Maal.

10. The idea that a basti is not a museum, unless the basti people want it to be so - was based on the authors observations from the film "Gully Boy"

11. The acting course that Anuradha mentions is at "Lee Strasberg Theatre & Film Institute" and are taken from the author's personal experience at the same institute.

12. The lyrics "Bhagawaan humare hai" contributed by Mohit Lal

13. Chimes of India is named after the news daily https://timesofindia.indiatimes.com

14. 96.4 spice FM is a radio channel in Bangladesh, know more here - "Spice FM - Wikipedia."

15. The line in the book "To make them understand is not only difficult but also impossible" is inspired by a dialogue from a Hindi film title "Don"

16. Lyrics - Chaar Botal Vodka are from rapper Yo Yo Honey Singh's song.

17. Read about Ozu and his camera angle here - www.quod.lib.umich.edu - Ozu and the poetics of cinema / David Bordwell..

18. Read about the hand gesture that Manoj makes here - "About: Baba Ji Ka Thullu - DBpedia."

19. Daya and Pradyuman are characters from a long running tv series titled - CID

20. The author mentions her personal experiences of acting in film and theatre when she meets Prem Ratan at his office to tell him that she is not going to act in his film.
21. Lyrics - ..kaha se gori ankhon mai pyaar leke, dilli sheher ka saara meena bazaar leke.. From - "Kajra Mohabbat Waala - Shamshad Begum"
22. Description of Prem Ratan's office based on the author's observations from the time she visited a film director's house at Versova, Bombay.
23. The author got to know about the actor Meena Kumari's real name in conversation with her aunt who the author thinks is almost a wikipedia on films and TV.
24. The Viral Fever - Bollywood Aam Aadmi Party : Arnub's Qtiyapa.
25. Film 'Sorcerer' for poster inspiration.
26. Mandi (Film) 1983 - for research on hyper-realism.
27. Film 'Shame', Al Jazeera documentaries & Batman Black and White for notes on lighting/cinematography.
28. Music from the Concert for Bangladesh organised by former Beatles lead guitarist George Harrison and Ravi Shankar.
29. How poetry became a crime in Assam by Samrat
30. Revolution Highway - Dilip Simeon
31. Assam's Bengal origin Muslims choose poetry to confront stereotypes and prejudices by M Reyaz
32. When Assam's Indigenous Muslims Threw in Their Lot With the BJP By Anuraag Baruah
33. Who are the Muslims of Assam? By Yasmin Saikia
34. Isn't 'Illegal Bangladeshi' Racist Shorthand for Bengali Speaking Muslims in Assam? Bonojit Hussain
35. Invisible immigrant by Sushanta Talukdar
36. National Register of Citizens in Assam: Issue of illegal foreigners continues to be a major political one by G Seetharaman
37. The Assam Gazette - June. 23rd, 1999
38. Assam - the Silent Genocide - Youtube Video
39. An overview of migration in India, its impacts and key issues - Ravi Srivastava and SK Sasikumar

40. Indian Nationality Law - Wikipedia
41. National Register of Citizens (NRC) | ASSAM GOVERNMENT Online Portal
42. Vajpayee-Advani imagined an all-India NRC and Modi-Shah added a Muslim filter - SHIVAM VIJ - The Print
43. Bangladesh Liberation War - Wikipedia
44. Demographic trends that are shaping the U.S. and the world by D'Vera Cohn and Andrea Caumont
45. BJP is Using Citizenship Act Amendment to Reinforce and Spread Hindutva in Assam by Hiren Gohain
46. Nation state boundaries and human rights of people in South Asia 1 Shomona Khanna
47. Cattle Smuggling Along Indo-Bangla Border: MHA Tells SC 1.7 Lakh Seizures In 2016; 35 Deaths, 302 Injured In Skirmish Since 2014.
48. An inside look on cattle smuggling at Bangladesh border - Kamaljit Kaur Sandhu
49. Fencing off Bangladesh - Delwar Hussain
50. BSF again kills Bangladeshi - The Daily Star
51. The Nowhere People - Rimple Mehta
52. Bangladeshi Migrants in India: Foreigners, Refugees, or Infiltrators? - Rizwana Shamshad
53. Who are the Rohingya boat people? The Telegraph
54. Why Human Rights Fail to Protect Undocumented Migrants - Gregor Noll

ON ASSAM, BANGLADESH; REFERENCES TO MIGRATION, CITIZENSHIP; IN CONTEXT WITH STRUCTURAL AND SYSTEMIC VIOLENCE:

1. To read more about a Sapori - riverine island - Quora." 31 May. 2018, What is a riverine island?.
2. To read more on "Concentration of Char Areas in Different Districts of Assam ...." Fig. 12: Concentration of Char Areas in Different Districts of Assam.
3. To read about the Sapori people's plight - "The 'river people' under threat - BBC Future."
4. Read about - "Bangladesh's dynamic coastal regions and sea-level rise ...." here - www.sciencedirect.com

5. Read about - "Miya people - Wikipedia."
6. Read about the CID's that are hired to detect Bangladeshis - www.thenewsminute.com - article - The uncertain future of the Bangladeshi immigrants taken from Bengaluru to Kolkata.
7. To read about who the D-voters are -
    a. "New NRC order on descendants of D-voters - The Hindu."
    b. "Narratives of D-voters in Assam – TwoCircles.net."
8. The register that Bano is referring to is - "Assam NRC final list out: What will happen to the 19 lakh excluded people?"
9. Read more about why some people fear immigrants and want them deported and/or blocked - Deport illegal immigrants as they pose security threat: Government - The Economic Times
10. Read more about why people assume that the waste-pickers are Bangladeshi immigrants here - Democracy, Citizen and Migrants Nationalism in the Era of Globalization (CCPD) – 2005
11. Read about how much the waste-pickers are asked to pay each time the cops come to catch them as Bangladeshis - Deportations of Bengali-speaking Muslims from Mumbai - Nivedita Rao, Simmy Kaur, Pravin Rana, et al.
12. Read about why the cop called Anuradha a "Bangladeshi thief" - "global migration perspectives - Refworld." GLOBAL MIGRATION PERSPECTIVES.
13. To know why Bano wants to sit on the floor -
    a. "'Tell Everyone We Scalped You!' How Caste Still Rules in India. - The New York Times."
14. And to read about caste-based work in India - "Safai Karmachari Andolan: Home."
15. Read about the Caste system in India and its association with leaving the waste-pickers smelling without letting them have access to clean water - "Caste system in India - Wikipedia."

16. Shimul Prodhan reference and the shooting of others from - www.theguardian.com/commentisfree/2009/sep/05/bangladesh-india-border-fence

17. Anuradha mentions to Bano that her father saw his brothers head get chopped off, that was taken from the author's conversation with a friend whose father saw this happen to his brother.

18. Dilip Simeon shared with the author that the issues of a migrant has great contemporary relevance not only in India, all over the world.

19. The Spectre Of "Hindu Bangladeshi" - Jyotirmoy Prodhani

20. 1971 - A Global History of The Creation of Bangladesh - Srinath RaghavanIndifference, impotence, and intolerance: transnational Bangladeshis in India - Sujata Ramachandran

21. Deportations of Bengali-speaking Muslims from Mumbai - Nivedita Rao, Simmy Kaur, Pravin Rana, et al.

22. Immigrant Detention Centres In India — Need For Transparency: Paresh Hate

23. Publications of Citizens Campaign for Preserving Democracy

24. The dark side of humanity and legality: A glimpse inside Assam's detention centres for 'foreigners' Scroll.in

25. Partition, Migration, and Jute Cultivation in India by Prashant Bharadwaj, James E. Fenske.

26. Inhumane Conditions in Assam Detention Camps, Alleges NELECC Civil Society - The Wire

27. 'What's Going On Is Really Unfair': Inside The Foreigners Tribunals In Assam - Huffpost

28. Case Closed by Sagar on The Caravan

29. The Voice of Dissent - A student led initiative in association with the Students' Council, Gargi College 2019-20

30. December 9, 2010. "Trigger Happy" Excessive Use of Force by Indian Troops at the Bangladesh Border

31. India/Bangladesh: Indiscriminate Killings, Abuse by Border Officers

32. Life and death in the Bangladesh-India margins Delwar Hussain 2 March 2009
33. History and politics of immigration of Muslims in Assam chapter 2
34. Bangladeshi Domestic Helpers in Delhi: A Study of Securitization of Migration in India and Its Impact on Bangladeshi Irregular Female Migrant Workers - Tasneem Siddiqui
35. The UN Refugee Agency Website
36. India, largely a country of immigrants - The Hindu, January 12, 2011
37. Report on 'Illegal' migration into Assam by the Governor of Assam. 8 November, 1998
38. Marichjhapi Incident - wikipedia
39. When Karnataka faced its own refugee crises and rose to the occasion - By Kushala S, Bangalore Mirror Bureau | Jan 31, 2016
40. Bengali Muslim - Wikipedia
41. Tales from a refugee land by Sneha Bengani
42. Raichur's Bangla Camps Struggling to Move On - article Times Of India Feb 1, 2016
43. ISIL Yearbook of International Humanitarian and Refugee Law
44. Fisheries in Tungabhadra Basin, India
45. Assam's Nellie Muslims say their vote was to stay back in India.
46. Dhaka, bangladesh: Walking Between Slums and dreamworlds.
47. Burmese and Bangladeshi refugees stranded in Bay of Bengal - The Telegraph
48. The Myth of the Bangladeshi and Violence in Assam: Nilim Dutta.
49. The Ghosts of Nellie, Assam: Thirty Years After; July 1, 2012; By Debarshi Das.
50. Muslims of Nellie village in Assam pin hopes on BJP after 'betrayal' by Congress, AGP by SV Krishnamachari.
51. Bengalis Bear the Brunt of Linguistic Polarisation Ahead of Assam Elections by Divya Guha

52. India Pakistan and the Secret Jihad - Praveen Swami

SAHYOG KENDRA TAKEN FROM AUTHORS EXPERIENCE WORKING AT HAZARDS CENTRE:

1. Sahyog Kendra is based on Hazards Centre - read more about it here - www.hazardscentre.org.
2. The description of Sahyog Kendra and the characters there are all based on the authors observations and experience working at Hazards Centre.
3. The painting of the cow at hazards Centre has a reference to a real painting at a friend's place of the authors.
4. The poster that Firoza is working on at hazards Centre is based on the lines taken from - "What Is Diversity, Inclusion and Belonging? | Nasdaq."
5. Midori's character is based on a person who approached Hazards Centre for her study on homeless women living on the streets.
6. Priyanka was a colleague of the authors at Hazards Centre
7. The interviews with the homeless immigrants mentioned in the book are based on:
    a. the authors experience while she interviewed the homeless women, and was translating for the
    b. researcher who approached Hazards Centre.
    c. The conversations about it are from conversations the author had at Hazards Centre with Dunu, Ranjan,
    d. Mukesh da and the researcher.
8. Tahir bhai's character is based on the life of someone who was living on the street and met Dunu Roy who supported him, the name of the character is also the name of a friend of the author.
9. Shambhuji is a colleague of the authors at Hazards Centre
10. The lyrics, "Swacch Bharat ka irada, ye irada kar liya humne.." are taken from the BJP governments Swachh

Bharat Campaign - translation - a clean India is our intention, we intend to make this happen..

11. The character Zublin is based on Mukesh da, who the author worked with at hazards Centre.

12. The concept of "do something" for the poor/society, is taken from the paper by Dunu Roy titled - Dogma and Debate.

13. Read more about why a slum is called a "gandi basti" here - dirty slum - FOR CONTEXT - "Dunu Roy: 'Slum Communities and Transformative Governance' | PRISM 2015- YouTube."

14. Read more about the study on the agency of homeless children why they choose to leave their homes and live on railway stations in India - "Life World and Agency of - AIWG-RCCR." http://www.rccr.in/upload/RCCR_Report_2019.pdf

15. Watch a workshop by Dunu Roy on Cops and Kids and their game of agency here - Facebook - Hazards Centre Videos - Cops & Kids - Game of Agency

16. Read about the safety hazards when Bangladesh gets annually flooded during the months of June to September.

17. Group 'Chalo" in the book is based on "LILA PRISM | LILA Foundation for Translocal Initiatives."

18. The conversation between Vikram and Zublin about people visiting basti's is taken from a group conversation at Hazard Centre regarding the artists from Art for Change visiting the waste-pickers basti at Gazipur.

19. Search and read about an Indian cop - Kiran devi who Guru bhai compares Kiran devi with, for being sturdy and the only women to venture out of the basti.

20. Read about what Anuradha means when she mentions safe workplace to Jina here -   Safe Worker, or Safe Workplace? Report by Hazards Centre

21. Read why the author mentions that the working class in India are the most connected to the ground - www.epw.in - journal - 2015/31 - perspectives - A Subaltern View of Climate Change.

22. The author's dream sequence is based on - "Petition update · GDA bulldozes the Gazipur slum · Change.org." Petition update · GDA bulldozes the Gazipur slum.
23. The quote "Work, education, rights do not make people poor, power does" is by Dunu Roy, the author added a few more words to it.
24. Slum Communities and Transformative Governance - Dunu Roy
25. Dogma and Debate - Dunu Roy

KAMAAL KI BASTI REFERENCES, CHARACTERS AND CONVERSATIONS BASED ON:
1. The real life experience of the author there
2. And with communities and colleagues working with Hazards Centre
3. And from conversations with
    a.   the real people there
    b.   and with Dunu Roy, Bali Charan
    c.   and the people who attended an art residency organised by Art for Change in Delhi in 2015.
4. Guru bhai's character is based on Bali Charan aka Bali bhai, and his experiences/narratives to the author.
5. Kamaal ki Basti - is the name given to the Waste-pickers basti near Radisson Blu, Kaushambi
6. Know more and/or contact the Waste-pickers Welfare Foundation here - "Waste-pickers Welfare Foundation - Home | Facebook."
7. Author learnt that immigrants come for livelihoods in conversation with Bengali-speaking immigrants at Seemapuri
8. Read about the Gazipur landfill here - Medium - The Logical Indian - 'Mount Everest Of Garbage' In Ghazipur, Delhi Is Causing Respiratory & Other Sickness Among Locals.
9. The description of the Gazipur landfill are from the authors visit to Ghazipur Landfill

10. Read about how the waste-pickers collect garbage braving the hazards of a landfill - "India's waste pickers brave landfills to live - Reuters." 22 Nov. 2011

11. Read about the hazards to the waste-pickers health here - "Household waste and health risks affecting waste pickers and ...." www.ncbi.nlm.nih.gov - pmc - articles

12. Chayapuri is the name given to Seemapuri (Delhi Assembly constituency) by the author. Chayapuri is based on the author's experience of visiting there and meeting with the waste-pickers and interviewing them there.

13. Watch The Kids Surviving Off Trash Dumps - YouTube." 26 Jul. 2015., Meet The Kids Surviving Off Trash Dumps.

14. Read why garbage is considered gold - www.thebetterindia.com - Here's How This NGO is Helping Ghazipur's Waste Pickers Get Gold From 'Garbage'.

15. Mahatoji's character is based on a real person from the waste-pickers basti at Gazipur

16. Read an interesting article on - how-namaste-flew-away-from-us - www.npr.org - sections

17. Author mentions many patterns created by the mesh pieces lying around in the basti that are created by waste that the better off discard, as she can she the beauty in what we think is useless/dirty even.

18. When Guru bhai mentions that the lawyers are getting a stay order - www.quora.com/What-is-a-the-meaning-of-a-court-stay-order

NONVIOLENT COMMUNICATION REFERENCES, LEARNINGS AND FURTHER READING SUGGESTIONS:

1. Read about - Observations Without Evaluations - Rainbow in Clouds - NVC 2 - Making Observations with Evaluations

2. Dialogue between Vikram and the young boy at the workshop organised by Chalo in the book, are inspired from the conversation mentioned in the book -

Nonviolent Communication - A Language of Life by Marshall B Rosenberg

3. To know more about the needs that are mentioned in several conversations in the book look at - NVC Needs Inventory

4. When Anuradha mentions that she wants to get to know the basti people without any questions of her own, she is referring to "Empathic listening with 'NVC ears' read more about it at Beyond the Right Words."

5. When Zublin gives Anuradha a compliment she points him to his needs, read why here - Compliments and praise, for their part, are tragic expressions of fulfilled needs - Nonviolent Communication - free resources - NVC social media quotes.

6. When someone appears weary of discussion to avoid discussion - read more how to embrace conflict here - Mediate.com - articles - NVC Conflict Coaching

7. Read what Manoj is lacking that makes him tell on Anuradha to teach his mother a lesson -   https://www.brainyquote.com/quotes - "Brene Brown - A deep sense of love and belonging is an...."

8. Authors understanding on Anuradha looking within to connect with needs of the cop that slaps her learnt at Nonviolent Communication Practise Group from CNVC Facilitator Sudha Shankar and from Sarah Peyton's webinar on Rage as a life serving force.

9. Know more about NVC grief and mourning - http://mindfulneeds.com/challenges/grief/

10. Read more about - Reflective listening - Wikipedia.

11. Read about why Anuradha raises her voice to match Nimrits tone - NVC Scream: Express intense emotions truthfully and nonjudgmentallyNVC (Nonviolent Communication) in Real Life.

12. When Anuradha goes inwards and hears a whisper - www.nonviolentcommunication.com - What's My Intention? A Simple Nonviolent Communication Exercise.   www.nvcindia.org/connection-before-education

13. When Anuradha puts back the focus on Shamuli - Marshall Rosenberg NVC Quote - Compliments and praise, for their part, are tragic expressions of fulfilled needs

14. What Anuradha suggests Shamuli to do for responding instead of reacting, is the author's learning at her Nonviolent Communication Practise Group Delhi from Sudha Shankar

15. To understand what shared realities are- www.mindfulneeds.com/specific-needs/shared-reality

16. Tit-for-tat is not fair/justice for all - www.jo-mchale.com/wp-content/uploads/2017/01/Honest-authentic-living-How-NVC-helps.pdf.

17. Blame and shame - "Can we talk? Nonviolent Communication (NVC)." https://www.cdss.org/images/organizers-resources/4-Can-We-Talk.pdf.

18. Read more about power with instead of power over - "Transforming Power Relations - Nonviolent Communication." https://www.nonviolentcommunication.com/pdf_files/power_relations_mkashtan.pdf.

19. Author was told by a friend when the author was crying, "Never stop crying" adding that is what the friend heard Miki Kashtan say.

20. More about shared realities that the author is referring to in the longing she put out with this book - Shared Reality - www.mindfulneeds.com/specific-needs

21. Nonviolent Communication - A Language of Life - Marshall B Rosenberg

22. Healing from the Blame that Binds by Kelly Bryson, MA, MFT

23. Internal Family Systems - An Introduction by Richard C Shwartz

24. Introduction: Nonviolence and NVC - www.cnvc.org

REFERENCES REGARDING DETENTION CENTRE IN THE NOVELLA:
1. Observations from authors visit to the Ren Basera/ Baraat Ghar at Shahazada Bagh, (near Shastri Nagar

Metro Station) that serves as a place for detaining alleged "illegal" migrants in 2015 - refer:

  a. Urban Governance Resistance - Democracy Citizenship - www.hazardscentre.org
  b. CCPD, Democracy, Citizens, and Migrants Nationalism in the era of Globalisation - Citizens' Campaign for
  c. Preserving Democracy
  d. Deportations of Bengali-speaking Muslims from Mumbai - Nivedita Rao, Simmy Kaur, Pravin Rana, et al.
  e. From the author's interview of homeless women for a Japanese researcher at the Hazards Centre.
  f. Read more about - Delhi Shelter - Ren Basera - www.delhishelterboard.in

2. With Reference to why Ameena wants to go back to Bangladesh -

  a. Indian girls women trafficked brides sexual domestic slavery - www.theguardian.com

3. Constable asks the other constable to stop weeping like a whore - in India there is a slang associated with it "randi rona " author is referring to that.

4. The part in the book where the constable talks about his hand being covered in blood is inspired by Shakespeare's Macbeth

5. Reason why the constable mentions that washing hands in the river Yamuna of Delhi will burn the other constables hand - Delhi air pollution creates toxic foam on Yamuna river - www.indiatoday.in

6. FRRO is the Foreigner Regional Registration Offices in India

7. Rajesh vs State on 22 April, 2011 Author: Mr.S.J.Mukhopadhaya

8. 'The people speak out: police harassment of Bengali-speaking Muslims of Yamuna Pushta'

9. Narratives of D-voters in Assam by Anjuman Ara Begum.

10. The Samatha Judgment and the Fifth Schedule of the
    Constitution - socialissuesindia.wordpress.com
11. When Anwar Miya speaks about having no other choice,
    reference the author's conversation with protestors at
    Shaheen Bagh, what the author heard them say about
    why they were sitting there.

CONVERSATION AT THE NEWSROOM DEBATE BASED ON
CONTENT FROM -

1. Beyond poll rhetoric BJP's contentious citizenship
   amendment bill - Kanchan Gupta - www.orfonline.org
2. India-Bangladesh border to be completely sealed by
   2018 Rajnath Singh - www.m.economictimes.com
3. Illegal immigration to India - Wikipedia
4. Bjp Election 2019 Manifesto English - DocumentCloud.
   Page 11
5. "The Broken Middle - Dilip Simeon's blog." 1 Nov. 2014,
   suggestions from Dilip Simeon
6. "Smriti Irani Powerful Speech in Parliament - YouTube."
   29 Apr. 2015
7. www.m.economictimes.com/news/defence/india-
   bangladesh-border-to-be-completely-sealed-by-
   mid-2018-rajnath-singh
8. www.downtoearth.org.in/coverage/governance/
   indigenous-people-in-india-and-the-web-of-indifference
9. CHAPTER I INTRODUCTION 1.1. Introduction Tripura,
   one of the smallest states of the Indian union is located
   in North- East India
10. www.dilipsimeon.blogspot.com/2019/09/sally-weale-
    finnish-education-system-is
11. Calibrated Indifference: Understanding the Structure of
    Informal Labour in India - www.sacw.sacw.info/article
12. The Newshour Debate: Modi's immigrant card, "The
    Handbook of Diasporas
    Media, and Culture | Wiley" - www.youtube.com
13. Urban Poverty and Informality: A Case Study of Okhla
    Assembly - www.amanpanchayat.org

14. Work undone: How India fails its young job seekers - www.aljazeera.com/news

15. India Working: Essays on Society and Economy - Barbara Harriss-White - www.books.google.com

16. Urban Poverty and Informality: A Case Study of Okhla Assembly - www.amanpanchayat.org

17. Does Amit Shah even understand what NRC will cost? - www.nationalheraldindia.com

18. The India-Bangladesh Wall: Lessons for Trump - www.thediplomat.com Democracy, Citizen and Migrants Nationalism in the Era of Globalization (CCPD) – 2005

19. Durga Ashtami is a Bengali religious festival.

20. The Newshour Debate: Modi's immigrant card - Full Debate (5th May 2014)- Arnub Goswami

THE CONVERSATION THAT ANURADHA HAS WITH HER FRIENDS FROM Bangalore ARE BASED ON:

1. The author's own experience with her friends.

2. Don't blame Wahabism for terrorism - www.nytimes.com

3. Why Nimrit chooses to not eat non-veg food on tuesdays - Why is eating non-vegetarian food a sin in Hindu religion - www.daily.bhaskar.com

4. Who the term "bhakt" is used for and why - A bhakt decodes the Modi phenomenon - www.rediff.com

5. English language in Europe - www./en.wikipedia.org

6. Getting beat up by police in Saudi countries - Human rights in Saudi Arabia - www.en.wikipedia.org

7. Hindutva - Wikipedia

8. To read about lynching in India - Tis is it. I'm going to die. India's minorities are targeted in lynchings - www.npr.org

9. Power over by instilling fear - A 10-step plan for turning a democracy into a dictatorship, from Robert Reich.

10. Aryans - RSS Rolls On Nazi Racist Project Of Producing 'Aryan' Babies In India.

11. Ban on English films in Bangalore - Authors experience in Bangalore - remembering when Plaza theatre wasn't

allowed to screen english language films for many weeks after its release.

12. www.sas.upenn.edu- "Kannada "Endangerment" - University of Pennsylvania.

13. Linguistic fight for states in India - Page 36 - "Bjp Election 2019 Manifesto English - DocumentCloud."

14. Is Kannada "Endangered"? H. Schiffman, South Asia Studies, University of Pennsylvania

15. Kannada, threatened at home - The Economist

16. Bengaluru: Pro-Kannada group demands removal of Hindi boards, threatens to blacken them - India Today

17. NRC will be rolled out across the country before 2024 polls: Amit Shah - Shaswati Das - livemint

MIXED REFERENCES, CONTEXTS, OTHERS:

1. The character Anuradha is loosely based on:
   a. the author
   b. and a friend of the authors - Ranjan Chakraborty

2. If you would like a glimpse into a typical South Indian lifestyle and influences:
   a. To view a picture of the wooden swing hanging in Anuradha's drawing room visit - Wooden Decor Swing - www.woodenswingshop.com
   b. To view a plantation chair visit - Traditional indian home in Coorg. planters chair. interior design. home design. color. decorating. architect. concrete floors. India desi....
   c. To know more about - the Kuchipudi dance form - "Kuchipudi - Wikipedia." "Tabla - Wikipedia."

3. CID is the "Criminal Investigation Department (India). Read about it at - Wikipedia."

4. When Anuradha is travelling on road in New Delhi:
   a. 'Dilli bole dil se, odd-even fir se.' was the tagline for the AAP governments odd-even campaign to reduce pollution from fuel smoke emission.
   b. The bus incident is the author's real experience using buses from Saket to Munirka in Delhi. One

of her colleagues even fractured her foot because the bus didn't halt at her stop, and she had to jump off a running bus to get off.

c. You could get a glimpse of the dome of the Islamic centre here - Abstract Islamic tile art from the various shrines of Uch Sharif - www.pinterest.com

d. Read about the traffic situation at Saket due to the malls here -

e. End to traffic nightmare outside the malls in Saket - www.hindustantimes.com

5. Who is gaining from illegal wildlife trade? Inside Story 25 May 2016 03:39 GMT Environment, Europe, Wildlife

6. India was a land of dharma but Europeans reduced it to Hinduism, Islam. And we accepted it - www.theprint.in

7. To understand Nonviolence, Punishment and Justice through - Nonviolent Communication Restorative Justice Circle, Belinda Hopkins, Annett Zupke, Joy of Living - Auroville - L'aura Joy and other NVC facilitators and practitioners.

8. Delhi violence Mandir-Masjid Marg - www.indianexpress.com

9. Meet Muslim man who helped group of Hindus to reach safer locations during Delhi riots - www.indiatimes.com

10. Woman got past rioters rescued 40 trapped relatives via rooftops - www.timesofindia.indiatimes.com

11. Sikhs, Muslims End 10-Year-Old Saharanpur Land Dispute - www.thequint.com

12. Northeast Delhi violence Gurdwaras open relief camp - www.indiatvnews.com

13. The scientifically proven, step-by-step guide to having a breakthrough conversation across party lines - By Lila MacLellan

14. Shahs Police blocking road to Shaheen Bagh - www.indianthinks.com

15. The Hindu critique of Hindutva - Avijit Pathak

16. A Brief History of the Sampradayikta Virodhi Andolan (SVA) - www.dilipsimeon.blogspot.in

17. CONSTITUTION OF the Sampradayikta Virodhi Andolan 1989 - - www.dilipsimeon.blogspot.in

18. Political Resolution of the Annual Convention of the Sampradayikta Virodhi Andolan, Delhi, March 1992 - www.dilipsimeon.blogspot.in

19. SVA Press Statement dtd 24 October 1990, following the arrest of LK Advani - www.sacw.net

20. Political Resolution of the Annual Convention of the SVA, Delhi, March 1992 - www.dilipsimeon.blogspot.in

21. The Broken Middle - on the 30th anniversary of 1984 - www.dilipsimeon.blogspot.in

22. मध्य मार्ग का अवसान : दिलीप सिमियन - www.dilipsimeon.blogspot.in

23. Sulphur in the air: 1984 is not forgotten - www.dilipsimeon.blogspot.in

24. PUDR Report: Who Are the Guilty? - www.pudr.org

25. A Hard Rain Falling - private armies & political violence in India - www.dilipsimeon.blogspot.in

26. Terrifying implications of the Staines judgement - www.dilipsimeon.blogspot.in

27. Modi Government worried after worst communal riots in decades in Delhi - www.thequint.com

28. India was a land of Dharma but Europeans reduced it to Hinduism Islam and we accepted it - www.theprint.in

29. The violence in Delhi politics and heroism of the ordinary - www.kafila.online

30. Shanti sena Gandhi peacekeeping army communal - www.thebetterindia.com

31. AHOM KINGDOM - WIKIPEDIA

32. ASSAM PROVINCE AND ASSAM STATE:
    a. HISTORY OF ASSAM - WIKIPEDIA
    b. Hindutva before Savarkar: Chandranath Basu's contribution - www.dnaindia.com
    c. Assam and the CAA: A Timeline from 1947 to the Assam Accord - NEWSCLICK.IN
    d. CULTIVATION IN ASSAM - IMMIGRATION AND ITS IMPACT ON ASSAM by Tapashi Gupta
    e. Assam Province - Wikiwand

f. AGRICULTURE - GROW MORE FOOD - "Revisiting Partition: Gandhi's Role in Integrating the ... - The Wire." 9 Aug. 2017, Revisiting Partition: Gandhi's Role in Integrating the Northeast with Independent India.

g. Assam Movement - Wikipedia

h. Attacks on Bengali-Muslims in Assam - Assam live: CM says govt to institute judicial inquiry into attacks - Aaron Pereira

i. Assam Border:

    i. History and Objectives - www.police.assam.gov.in

    ii. Making of India's Northeast: Geopolitics of Borderland and Transnational Interactions - Dilip Gogoi

    iii. Border Security Force - Wikipedia

33. ANGLO-BURMESE WAR:

a. THE SIR ARTHUR PHAYRE COLLECTION OF BURMESE MANUSCRIPTS. pp. 237.

b. WIKIPEDIA

34. BRITISH ADMINISTRATIVE POLICIES: REORGANISATION OF BENGAL: ITS IMPACTS:

a. Partition of Bengal (1905) - Wikipedia

b. DIVIDE AND RULE - Chandra, Bipan. History of Modern India, ISBN 978-81-250-3684-5, pp. 248–249

c. BRITISH RAJ - WIKIPEDIA

d. Establishment of All India Muslim League - Story of Pakistan. p. 1.

e. TWO NATION THEORY - "The Sole Spokesman Jinnah, the Muslim League and ... - Home." The Sole Spokesman Jinnah, the Muslim League and the Demand for Pakistan.

35. PARTITION, EXODUS, CITIZENSHIP, timeline since 1947:

a. FOREIGNERS ACT - Democracy, Citizen and Migrants Nationalism in the Era of Globalization (CCPD) – 2005

b.   Illegal Migration into Assam - www.satp.org

c.   A Brief History of the Sampradayikta Virodhi Andolan (SVA) - www.dilipsimeon.blogspot.in

d.   Video: History of CAA lies in the history of 1948: Abhinav Chandrachud - www.sacw.net

e.   The Indo-Pakistani War of 1965 - wikipedia

f.   Indian nationality law - Wikipedia

g.   "NRC timeline through the years - The Economic Times." 2 Jan. 2020, National Register of Citizens: NRC timeline through the years.

h.   Citizenship (Amendment) Act, 2019 - Wikipedia

i.   Politics and Development in India - Raghu Mahajan - wordpress.com

j.   1951 Census of India - Wikipedia

k.   IMDT ACT - On Supreme Court's Verdict On IMDT Act - People's Democracy

l.   Mukul Kesavan Sulphur in the air 1984 - www.dilipsimeon.blogspot.com

m.   A brief history of Assam, Assam Movement & Assam Accord and the implementation of NRC & CAA - www.northeasttoday.in

n.   Assam final NRC list released: 19,06,657 people excluded, 3.11 crore make it to citizenship list - www.indiatoday.in

o.   The Voice of Dissent - A student led initiative in association with the Students' Council, Gargi College 2019-20

About the Author

Menaka is a Nonviolent Communication (NVC) Practitioner which is based on the work of Marshall B. Rosenberg. She has attended workshops by certified NVC facilitators Miki Kashtan, Sudha Shankar and others. Menaka continues to attend workshops and is actively part of the Delhi NVC Practice Group from the end of 2017, as she chooses to live in NVC consciousness.